THE MARGINALIZATION OF POETRY

BOB PERELMAN

The Marginalization of Poetry

Language Writing and
Literary History

PRINCETON UNIVERSITY PRESS, PRINCETON, NEW JERSEY

Copyright © 1996 by Princeton University Press
Published by Princeton University Press, 41 William Street, Princeton, New Jersey 08540
In the United Kingdom: Princeton University Press, Chichester, West Sussex

Library of Congress Cataloging-in-Publication Data

Perelman, Bob.
The marginalization of poetry : language writing and literary history / by Bob Perelman.
p.   cm.
Includes index.
ISBN 0-691-02139-2 (CL : alk. paper). — ISBN 0-691-02138-4 (PB : alk. paper)
1. American poetry—20th century—History and criticism—Theory, etc.
2. Language and languages in literature.   3. Poetics.   I. Title.
PS325.P37   1996
811'.509—dc20   95-26685

Permissions

Basil Bunting, "Molten pool, incandescent spilth of" from *Collected Poems* ©1994 by Basil
    Bunting, Oxford University Press by permission of Oxford University Press.
Robert Creeley, "One thing," "As real as thinking," "Again" from *The Collected Poems of
    Robert Creeley* ©1982 by Robert Creeley, University of California Press by permission of
    University of California Press.
Robert Grenier, poems from *Sentences* ©1978 by Robert Grenier, Whale Cloth Press and
    from *What I Believe   Transpirational/Transpiring   Minnesota* ©1989 Robert Grenier,
    O Press by permission of Robert Grenier.
Ted Berrigan, "Sonnet 15" from *The Sonnets* ©1964 by Ted Berrigan, Grove Press by
    permission of Alice Notley.
Lyn Hejinian, "Chapter Eighty-Nine" from *Oxota* ©1991 by Lyn Hejinian, The Figures Press
    by permission of The Figures Press.
Rae Armantrout, "The Garden," "Necromance," from *Necromance* ©1991 by Rae
    Armantrout, Sun & Moon Press by permission of Sun & Moon Press.
Susan Howe, "Thorow" from *Singularities* ©1990 by Susan Howe, Wesleyan University Press
    by permission of University Press of New England.
Frank O'Hara, "The Critic" and "Heroic Sculpture" from *Collected Poems* by Frank O'Hara,
    Copyright ©1981 and ©1970, respectively, by Maureen Granville-Smith, Administratrix
    of the Estate of Frank O'Hara. Reprinted by permission of Alfred A. Knopf, Inc.
Frank O'Hara, "A step away from them" Copyright ©1964 by Frank O'Hara. Reprinted by
    permission of City Lights.

This book has been composed in Times Roman

Princeton University Press books are printed on acid-free paper and meet the
guidelines for permanence and durability of the Committee on Production Guidelines
for Book Longevity of the Council on Library Resources

Printed in the United States of America by Princeton Academic Press

1 2 3 4 5 6 7 8 9 10

CONTENTS

ACKNOWLEDGMENTS

In 1990 I left the Bay Area for a job at the University of Pennsylvania. This book reflects that move: my longstanding engagement with language writing will be evident as well as my later involvement with the larger, compartmentalized pastures of the academy.

While I am clearly an interested party, I intend this as a critical book and not simply a celebration or an example of language writing. In places I've departed from the standard protocols of professional criticism: I would like the formal gestures to register as significant without sacrificing public legibility. We'll see.

I have tried to discuss some of the variety of language writing, but I have certainly not succeeded in dealing with or even mentioning many books and writers who deserve intricate response. Here, to reverse a phrase of Marianne Moore, omissions are accidents, deficiencies.

I owe my interest in writing to many writers. Among others, thanks, general and permanent thanks, to Lyn Hejinian, Barrett Watten, Ron Silliman, Carla Harryman, Charles Bernstein, Michael Davidson, Rae Armantrout, Kit Robinson, David Bromige, Robert Grenier, Bruce Andrews, Nate Mackey, Fanny Howe, Tom Mandel, the late Ted Berrigan, Robert Creeley, Michael Palmer, Susan Howe, Steve McCaffery, Leslie Scalapino, Norman Fischer, Jed Rasula, Abigail Child, James Sherry, Ben Friedlander, Jackson Mac Low, Larry Price, Joan Retallack, Peter Middleton, Donald Hall, Rod Smith, Jean Day, the late Jerry Estrin, Geoff Young, Kathleen Fraser, Clark Coolidge, David Melnick, Diane Ward, Eileen Corder, Alan Davies, Laura Moriarty, Erica Hunt, Alan Bernheimer, the late Larry Eigner, Anselm Hollo, Lisa Robertson, Rachel Blau DuPlessis, Susan Stewart, Gil Ott, Julia Blumenreich, Eli Goldblatt, and Noah DeLissovoy.

Specific thanks to Marjorie Perloff, who invited me to give a talk on "The Marginalization of Poetry"; to Susan Howe, who supplied encouragement, hints, and the word "marginalia"; to Jim English, who facilitated the piece's original appearance in *Postmodern Culture* and later in the book *Essays in Postmodern Culture*, edited by Eyal Amiran and John Unsworth; to James Sherry, whose Roof Press published it as a poem in *Virtual Reality*; to Peter Baker, who anthologized it in *Onward: Contemporary Poetry and Poetics*; and to Douglas Messerli, who anthologized it in *From the Other Side of the Century: A New American Poetry 1960–90*.

To Rod Smith, who published a version of "Language Writing and Literary

History" in the Barrett Watten issue of *Aerial*. This version also contained versions of the signifying-poems, which here are called "An Alphabet of Literary History." To Antoine Caze and Marie-Christine Lemardelay-Cunci, who published a portion of it in the *Revue Française d'Etudes Americaines*.

To Peter Stallybrass, Jean-Michel Rabaté, Margreta Degrazia, Stuart Curran, Al Filreis, Vicki Mahaffey, Phyllis Rackin, and Michael Ryan, who organized a series of seminars on the book at the University of Pennsylvania. The talk I gave there became "Here and Now On Paper."

To Cathy Davidson and Michael Moon, who published a version of "Parataxis and Narrative: The New Sentence in Theory and Practice" in *American Literature*; to Jerry Herron, who published it in *The Ends of Theory*, edited by Jerry Herron, Dorothy Huson, Ross Pudaloff, and Robert Strozier; and to Fredric Jameson, for supplying the original instigation.

To Rita Barnard, Herman Beavers, Dana Phillips, and Craig Saper, for comments on "Write the Power"; to Gordon Hutner, who published it in *American Literary History*.

To Tenney Nathanson, who published "Building a More Powerful Vocabulary: Bruce Andrews and the World (Trade Center)" in *The Arizona Quarterly*.

To the late Sherman Paul, who published an early portion of "This Page Is My Page, This Page Is Your Page: Gender and Mapping" in *The South Dakota Quarterly*.

And to Jean-Michel Rabaté, who asked me at the last second to come up with something "a little creative" for the "After Roland Barthes" conference organized by him and Craig Saper at the University of Pennsylvania in May 1994.

I also want to acknowledge a fellowship from the MacDowell Colony and a Research Foundation Grant from the University of Pennsylvania.

This book is dedicated to my wife, Francie Shaw; our children, Max and Reuben Perelman; and to the memory of my mother, Evelyn Strassels Perelman.

THE MARGINALIZATION OF POETRY

ONE

The Marginalization of Poetry

If poems are eternal occasions, then
the pre-eternal context for the following

was a panel on "The Marginalization
of Poetry" at the American Comparative

Literature Conference in San Diego, on
February 8, 1991, at 2:30 P.M.:

"The Marginalization of Poetry"—it almost
goes without saying. Jack Spicer wrote,

"No one listens to poetry," but
the question then becomes, who is

Jack Spicer? Poets for whom he
matters would know, and their poems

would be written in a world
in which that line was heard,

though they'd scarcely refer to it.
Quoting or imitating another poet's line

is not benign, though at times
the practice can look like flattery.

In the regions of academic discourse,
the patterns of production and circulation

are different. There, it—again—goes
without saying that words, names, terms

are repeatable: citation is the prime
index of power. Strikingly original language

is not the point; the degree
to which a phrase or sentence

fits into a multiplicity of contexts
determines how influential it will be.

"The Marginalization of Poetry": the words
themselves display the dominant *lingua franca*

of the academic disciplines and, conversely,
the abject object status of poetry:

it's hard to think of any
poem where the word "marginalization" occurs.

It is being used here, but
this may or may not be

a poem: the couplets of six-
word lines don't establish an audible

rhythm; perhaps they aren't, to use
the Calvinist mercantile metaphor, "earning" their

right to exist in their present
form—is this a line break

or am I simply chopping up
ineradicable prose? But to defend this

(poem) from its own attack, I'll
say that both the flush left

and irregular right margins constantly loom
as significant events, often interrupting what

I thought I was about to
write and making me write something

else entirely. Even though I'm going
back and rewriting, the problem still

reappears every six words. So this,
and every poem, is a marginal

work in a quite literal sense.
Prose poems are another matter: but

since they identify themselves as poems
through style and publication context, they

become a marginal subset of poetry,
in other words, doubly marginal. Now

of course I'm slipping back into
the metaphorical sense of marginal which,

however, in an academic context is
the standard sense. The growing mass

of writing on "marginalization" is not
concerned with margins, left or right

—and certainly not with its own.
Yet doesn't the word "marginalization" assume

the existence of some master page
beyond whose justified (and hence invisible)

margins the panoplies of themes, authors,
movements, objects of study exist in

all their colorful, authentic, handlettered marginality?
This master page reflects the functioning

of the profession, where the units
of currency are variously denominated prose:

the paper, the article, the book.
All critical prose can be seen

as elongated, smooth-edged rectangles of writing,
the sequences of words chopped into

arbitrary lines by the typesetter (Ruth
in tears amid the alien corn),

and into pages by publishing processes.
This violent smoothness is the visible

sign of the writer's submission to
norms of technological reproduction. "Submission" is

not quite the right word, though:
the finesse of the printing indicates

that the author has shares in
the power of the technocratic grid;

just as the citations and footnotes
in articles and university press books

are emblems of professional inclusion. But
hasn't the picture become a bit

binary? Aren't there some distinctions to
be drawn? Do I really want

to invoke Lukács's "antinomies of bourgeois
thought" where, rather than a conceptually

pure science that purchases its purity
at the cost of an irrational

and hence foul subject matter, we
have the analogous odd couple of

a centralized, professionalized, cross-referenced criticism studying
marginalized, inspired (i.e., amateur), singular poetries?

Do I really want to lump
The Closing of the American Mind,

Walter Jackson Bate's biography of Keats,
and *Anti-Oedipus* together and oppose them

to any poem which happens to
be written in lines? Doesn't this

essentialize poetry in a big way?
Certainly some poetry is thoroughly opposed

to prose and does depend on
the precise way it's scored onto

the page: beyond their eccentric margins,
both Olson's *Maximus Poems* and Pound's

Cantos tend, as they progress, toward
the pictoral and gestural: in Pound

the Chinese ideograms, musical scores, hieroglyphs,
heart, diamond, club, and spade emblems,

little drawings of the moon and
of the winnowing tray of fate;

or those pages late in *Maximus*
where the orientation of the lines

spirals more than 360 degrees—one
spiralling page is reproduced in holograph.

These sections are immune to standardizing
media: to quote them you need

a photocopier not a word processor.
Similarly, the work of writers

associated with the language movement avoids
standardized typographical grids and is as

self-specific as possible: Robert Grenier's *Sentences,*
a box of 500 poems printed

on notecards, or his recent holograph
work, often scrawled; the variable leading

and irregular margins of Larry Eigner's
poems; Susan Howe's writing, which uses

the page like a canvas—from
these one could extrapolate a poetry

where publication would be a demonstration
of singularity approximating a neo-Platonic vanishing

point, anticipated by Russian Futurist handcolored
book—Khlebnikov once read *The Temptation*

of Saint Anthony burning each page
for light to read the next—

Such an extrapolation would be inaccurate
as regards the writers I've mentioned,

and certainly creates a false picture
of the language movement, some of

whose members write very much for
a if not the public. But

still there's another grain of false
truth to my Manichean model of

a prosy command-center of criticism and
unique bivouacs on the poetic margins

so I'll keep this binary in
focus for another spate of couplets.

Parallel to such self-defined poetry, there's
been a tendency in some criticism

to valorize if not fetishize the
unrepeatable writing processes of the masters:

Gabler's *Ulysses*, where the drama of
Joyce's writing mind becomes the shrine

of a critical edition; the facsimile
of Pound's editing-creation of what became

Eliot's *Waste Land*; the packets into
which Dickinson sewed her poems, where

the sequences possibly embody a higher
order; the notebooks in which Stein

and Toklas conversed in pencil: these
can make works like "Lifting Belly"

seem like an interchange between bodily
writers or writerly bodies in bed.

The feeling that three's a crowd
there is called up then cancelled

by the print's intimacy and tact.
In all these cases, the unfathomable

particularity of the author's mind, body,
and writing situation is the illegible

icon of reading. But it's time
to dissolve this binary. What about

a work like *Glas*?—hardly a
smooth critical monolith. Doesn't it use

the avant-garde (ancient poetic adjective!) device
of collage more extensively than most

poems? Is it really that different
from, say, *The Cantos*? (Yes. *The*

Cantos's growing incoherence reflects Pound's free-fall
writing situation; Derrida's institutional address is

central. Unlike Pound's, Derrida's cut threads
always reappear farther along.) Nevertheless *Glas*

easily outstrips most contemporary poems in
such "marginal" qualities as undecidability and

indecipherability—not to mention the 4
to 10 margins per page. Compared

to it, these poems look like
samplers upon which are stitched the

hoariest platitudes. Not to wax polemical:
there've been numerous attacks on the

voice poem, the experience poem, the
mostly free-verse descendants of Wordsworth's spots

of time: first-person meditations where the
meaning of life becomes visible after

20 or 30 lines. In its
own world, this poetry is far

from marginal: widely published and taught,
it has established substantial means of

reproducing itself. But with its distrust
of intellectuality (apparently synonymous with overintellectuality)

and its reliance on authenticity as
its basic category of judgment (and

the poems exist primarily to be
judged) (with the award having replaced

aura in the post-canonical era of
literary reproduction), it has become marginal

with respect to the theory-oriented sectors
of the university, the sectors which

have produced such concepts as "marginalization."
As an antidote, let me quote

Glas: "One has to understand that
he is not *himself* before being

Medusa to himself. . . . To be oneself
is to-be-Medusa'd. . . . Dead sure of self. . . .

Self's dead sure biting (death)." Whatever
this might mean, and it's possibly

aggrandizingly post-feminist, man swallowing woman, nevertheless
in its complication of identity it

seems a step toward a more
communal and critical reading and writing

and thus useful. The puns and
citations lubricating Derrida's path, making it

too slippery for all but experienced
cake walkers, are not the point.

What I am proposing in these
anti-generic, over-genred couplets is not some

genreless, authorless writing, but a physically
and socially located writing where margins

are not metaphors, and where readers
are not simply there, waiting to

be liberated. Despite its transgression of
local critical decorum, *Glas* is, in

its treatment of the philosophical tradition,
decorous; it is *marginalia*, and the

master page of Hegel is still
Hegel, and Genet is Hegel too.

But a self-critical poetry, minus the
short-circuiting rhetoric of vatic privilege, might

dissolve the antinomies of marginality that
broke Jack Spicer into broken lines.

TWO

Language Writing and Literary History

Overthrowing and Entering Literary History

The opening and closing lines of the prior poem contain ironies that trouble me. Suggesting that "poems are eternal occasions" and giving the date of the Comparative Literature panel creates an opposition, however ironically poised, between poetry that is timeless and criticism that is set firmly, even fashionably, in history. Yet the poem wants to unite the two spheres, and it ends with the hope that "a self-critical poetry . . . might dissolve the antinomies of marginality"—that it might redraw or undo generic boundaries between poetry and criticism. By displaying its arbitrary form, the piece is willful in challenging distinctions, claiming that, as far as genre is concerned, the act of writing confers an automatic power of definition. But the conditional "might dissolve" registers the difficulties. The rifts between poetry and criticism, writing and theory, are not easily spanned. Literature and creative-writing departments are well-established regimes that generate a continuing proliferation of marginalities, antinomies, and linguistic specializations. The spread of the self-fashioning of genre envisioned by the poem depends on more than any single act of modeling: it needs to be supplemented by many acts in many contexts.

Literary history is normally a retrospective category of bureaucratic struggle and consensus, and not a site for active writing. Writers write and get sorted out later: good, bad, modernist, postmodernist, novelist, poet. But "The Marginalization of Poetry" wants to reconfigure the categories of literary history. As a performative gesture such a task is, of course, chancy: in this, it is perhaps typical of language writing. I immediately feel compelled to add that typicality is a sore point for many language writers. One of the projects of this book is to unravel recent received ideas of language writing as a uniform practice.

The poetic movement known as language writing or language poetry began to take shape in the San Francisco Bay Area in the early seventies and a few years later in New York City, with a smaller nexus in Washington, DC. While language writing has, by the mid-nineties become a recognized literary-historical term, there was never any self-consciously organized group known as the language writers or poets—not even a fixed name.

This fact has not prevented "language writing," as a polemic horizon pregnant with unknown but unwanted developments, from often being invoked over the last two decades. There are real reasons for this: the positive structures of language writing are socially and aesthetically complex and in places strained and contradictory, but the movement has been more united by its opposition to the prevailing institutions of American poetry. During this period, American poetry has been dominated by writing workshops and creative-writing departments with large networks of legitimation—publishing, awards, reviews, extensive university connections. The aesthetics of this mainstream are not without variation, but generalizations are possible, and were certainly made, polemically, by those involved in the formation of language writing: the mainstream poet guarded a highly distinct individuality; while craft and literary knowledge contributed to poetry, sensibility and intuition reigned supreme. The mainstream poet was not an intellectual and especially not a theoretician. Hostility to analysis and, later, to theory, were constitutive of such a poetic stance. In this situation, modernism was no longer especially important. The discursive tone of later Eliot, the incantatory vaticism of Yeats, the kaleidoscopic novelty of Surrealism minus Marx and Freud, the authoritative common sense and rural cast of Frost (often translated to the suburbs), and an attenuated version of Williams as poet of the quotidian—these echoes might be read everywhere, but the more basic facts of modernism were shunned. The poet as engaged, oppositional intellectual, and poetic form and syntax as sites of experiment for political and social purposes—these would not be found. The confessional poets were the model: Lowell, Plath, Sexton, Berryman. Poems were short, narrative, focused on small or large moments of crisis or optimism. Whether the form was free verse or rhymed iambic stanzas, the tone was conversational. Such work was often unambitious, and the steady production of books and MFA graduates bespoke a bureaucratized routine, but the breakdowns and suicides of the leading exemplars stood as guarantees of intensity.

The formation of language writing was given a negative impetus by such a poetic climate. The goals variously articulated by members of the group were quickly registered as hostile to the well-being of that climate. And this literary hostility was seen as emanating from a group of writers. Subsequent publications would show that "the group" was not often all that cohesive: influence and interaction never produced a uniform literary program, let alone a uniform style. But there was a loose set of goals, procedures, habits, and verbal

commonalities :

textures: breaking the automatism of the poetic "I" and its naturalized voice; foregrounding textuality and formal devices;[1] using or alluding to Marxist or poststructuralist theory in order to open the present to critique and change. These, along with the group interaction and the aggressive dismissals of self-expressive mainstream poetics as politically reactionary, raised the specter of a Lenin-esque cadre dedicated to the overthrow of poetry. Robert von Hallberg sees mainstream American poetry of this period as the poetry of accommodation; language writing coalesced as American involvement in Vietnam was nearing its bankrupt conclusion: this was a significant cause of the unaccommodating nature of its poetics. But linkages between poetry and politics were always the source of dispute. For some, language writing was too programmatically political to be poetry; for a number of New American poets and their supporters, it was too poststructuralist to be political.

Many features of this literary battle were reproduced on a wider scale by the introduction of poststructuralist thought into the American academy. While both were housed in universities, creative writing departments and English departments generally had nothing to do with one another; the advent of theory made the separation wider. Language writing was easy enough to subsume under the category of theory or postmodernism as part of a large tendency attacking self, reference, and history. As initial formal goals and polemical rallying cries, such attacks had specific literary value; as slogans they have devolved to little more than inflight snacks served on the proliferant hovercrafts of postmodernism.

The recent edition of *The New Princeton Encyclopedia of Poetry and Poetics* contains a short article on "Language Poetry" that sees it emerging as a "reaction to and outgrowth of . . . Black Mountain, New York School, and Beat" aesthetics.[2] The article appears between entries on "Landscape Poem" and "Langue": it is a minor piece of evidence that language writing has become a fact of literary history. But its placement makes a good place to start a description. It is just an alphabetic coincidence, but language writing finds itself between the still-dominant scenic monolog of the writing workshops and poststructuralist *langue*—between, in other words, claims that language is natural to the individual and claims that language is transindividual.[3] Another way to stage this division would be to place language writing between work that is poetry in an all-too-secure sense and work that pays little attention to the category of poetry.

The various practices that make up the provisional historical moment of language writing attempt to be autonomous, self-determining, free from the prior bureaucratic impositions of literary history. But at the same time, these impositions are hard to ignore. Whether they are called cultural capital or poetic traditions, they are also vital concerns, and they animate poets, critics, teachers, and constructors of high school, college, and graduate curricula and syllabi; they determine taste and literary judgment, which ultimately means they are crucial in determining the circulation of writing and the formation of future readers and writers. All attempts at literary autonomy are bound up with desires for outward effect, both political and poetic. In the latter case, the goal may be either to overthrow or to enter the poetic mainstream.

Given the long-delayed nature of most literary politics, these two alternatives become less oppositional. In the case of poetry especially, the history of what will later become the mainstream is one in which literary overthrow is a standard practice. The performance pieces and talks on poetics that took place frequently during the initial stages of the formation of the language group were communal events, casual, intense interactions that took place in lofts and art spaces. But they were not only addressed to immediate participants: they were also recorded. However contingent or trivial some of the remarks were, those tapes were aimed toward entering and redefining literary history. Ron Silliman may have concluded one critical piece with the Lenin-esque call to "undermine the bourgeoisie," but in another talk he would declare that he had been crucially influenced by the fiercely apolitical poetry of Jack Spicer.[4] The opposition is compactly expressed in Silliman's *Tjanting*: "This is how we came to resume writing, that we might free ourselves of literature."[5] "Literature" here is the hierarchical, bureaucratic sum of school, anthologies, curricula—what I am calling literary history; "writing" (for which I am reading "language writing") is both practice and utopia. But I find these two areas impossible to disentangle: the literary arena, which finally means the social arena, surrounds and constitutes each act of writing.

The political remarks have gotten more attention than the declarations of poetic heritage. Members of the group met and began working with some sense of connection in the early seventies; by the eighties, the group's interests in formal experiment and its politicized literary theorizing began to attract notice, positive and negative. Many poets and critics found the work to be overly intellectual, anathema to the model of intuitive self-expression then current—and still current. Subsequent publications would show that "the group" was not often all that cohesive: influence and interaction never produced a uniform style. But the interaction, the sometimes Marxist and always intellectual vocabulary, and the aggressive dismissals of self-expressive poetics raised the specter of a cadre of theoretical would-be poets for a number of readers. Even though almost all language writers were based outside the university, language writing was accused of being academic before very many academics had heard much about it. By the mid-eighties university critics began to take notice, attacking or celebrating the movement's literary-political claims; but the claims have tended to receive more consideration than the writing itself and the specific literary traditions it grew out of. Language writers have used structuralist and poststructuralist theory at times to furnish ad hoc support for negative assertions about the problematic status of description, self, and narrative in writing and positive ones about wider possibilities for meaning if more ambitious sets of reading practices are recognized; but these positions have come out of writing practices closely informed by the modernists, especially Stein, and the Objectivists, especially Zukofsky, and by Black Mountain, Beat, and New York School poetry. Thus—to be schematic about it—language writing occupies a middle territory bounded on the one side by poetry as it is currently instituted and on the other by theory. Language writing contests the expressive model emanating from workshops and creative-writing departments; but its potential rapprochement with poststructuralist theory and cultural studies has been slowed due to the specific histories of poetry it presupposes. The material bases of writing—letters, syntax, procedures—are glossed over by the workshop poem's commitment to voice and immediate experience; theoretical regimes generate critique through reading, whether the text is *Wuthering Heights* or weather reports, and the writing that maps out these readings tends to be subservient to institutionalized philosophic reference, often resulting in jargon. Language writing differs from both sides in foregrounding writing as an active process.

Rather than being a symptom of postmodernism, language writing fits into the sequence of twentieth-century avant-garde poetic movements, although it is by no means equivalent to any of them. The collective nature of the movement was crucial to the development of the writing, but it is difficult to define: later, I will be giving a somewhat anecdotal account of how things worked in practice. The shifting collectivities were somewhat amorphous, focused around specific venues and publications. The Objectivists, rather than firmly organized groups like the Surrealists or OULIPO, would be the closest antecedent. However, the Objectivists were an active collective for only a single period in the thirties: the "Objectivists" issue of *Poetry* and the mostly projected series of publications by To Press; later, the term became a literary-historical convenience to designate the work of several rather isolated writers. The language writers, on the other hand, have worked together or at least attended to one another's work closely for two decades.

Even in this schematic description, I'm finding tense to be a problem, especially when "language writing" is the subject. Should it be "Language writing differs" or "Language writing differed?" If language writing is defined as a literary movement involving a specific group of writers, I could use the past tense; if it is a generalizable set of concerns, then the present. The period of intense group interaction that began over twenty years ago is subsiding, although almost all those associated with the original writing scenes have continued to write. There is now a specific history that could be chronicled—books, magazines, venues, individual careers. But then again there is currently a great deal of literary activity arising elsewhere that could easily be called language writing. A young woman writing to Lyn Hejinian identified herself as one of "the language writers in Australia."[6] Here I will not be interested in adjudicating boundaries—although the existence of such imaginary boundaries is a charged literary fact.

A movement without specific manifestos or official membership will tend to be identified through the writing of some of its members: this is happening with language writing. A subsequent critical assessment may well focus on "major" or "representative" figures, but specific venues, magazines, and publishing ventures were important in forming the sense of a group project and making that project various. A coffee house in the Haight-Ashbery district of San Francisco, The Grand Piano, was the site of a long-running series of readings; a performance of Zukofsky's *"A"-24;*[7] and a production of a Frank O'Hara play, *Try! Try!* The Talk Series that I curated would include a presentation of Shklovsky and Russian Formalism, a meditation of open versus closed forms, or an improvized performance piece.[8]

The formation of self-managed literary venues is more obvious in the case of magazines: *This*, begun in 1971, *Hills* (1973), and *L=A=N=G=U=A=G=E* (1978) were initially significant. More than simply places to publish poems, they were sites for a deliberate cultivation of critical thinking, though the writing rarely displayed a professionalized evenness of surface. The first issue of *This* contained something like a manifesto by one of the editors, Robert Grenier, in which he polemicized against persona poems and the conversational first-person lyric. An issue of *Hills* published transcriptions of talks by language writers; *L=A=N=G=U=A=G=E* was a critical journal, although the categories of "criticism" and "poetry" were often hard to distinguish within the larger category of "writing." Nevertheless, many critical and informational projects were proposed in its pages such as "The Politics of the Referent," "Some Recent British Poetry Magazines," or a section on "Reading Stein."[9]

The development of presses—Lyn Hejinian's Tuumba chapbook series; Geoff Young's press, The Figures; Barrett Watten's This Press; James Sherry's Roof Press—established something of a complete literary environment for language writing. This development can be interpreted variously. The completeness of its self-management allowed for immediate access to publication and review, which in turn encouraged large-scale projects and formal variety.

Most importantly this created a sense that writing was public: breaking open new territory and entering and changing literary history seemed synonymous. But there was a reverse side to such autonomy: language writers were often accused of being a clique, writing for, reviewing, and publishing each other. Such characterizations can easily be applied to the poetic mainstream, of course. If looked at in detail, the publishing histories of the presses and magazines give evidence of a cohesive group with porous boundaries.

The initial phase of language writing is over; the careers of the participants continue; there is still widespread interest in and controversy over the issues that were raised. These issues were and are still being raised in specific, compelling acts of writing. The issues and the writing will be my concern here.

Group Labels

There are more poets in America than most poets and critics might care to think about, and they comprise a widely varied lot. But this variety occurs in a climate (or market) for poetry in which individuality and identity politics are dominant (and sometimes competing) possibilities. So it's no surprise that, both on a formal level and in terms of how the poet's function is defined, language writing has often been received as problematic by nonacademic poets and by critics. When Joel Lewis wrote an article about language writing for an issue of *Poets & Writers*, the next issue printed four letters attacking the movement. One writer complained of "disconnected phrases, avoiding communication," and said the movement should be called "Rambling Typists": "These poems are 'hard' if you try to find meaning. In fact the writing is so easy. The only difficulty is in avoiding connections that could be called insightful or profound. By stabbing with my pen at random words and phrases . . . in about a minute I 'wrote' this Language Poem:

> One rejection slip
> the list goes on
> it beats being ignored
> a carnival of public readings
> a bag of cement

Perhaps I've been struggling too hard over the years to make my poems make sense when nonsense is so easy."[10]

Here, the almost century-old technique of Dada composition again demonstrates its uncanny powers: the poem can be read as giving a usable account of the dynamics of the language movement. It begins in the landscape of the mainstream poetry world, dominated by the mysteries of aesthetic judgment, whose dread emblem is the rejection slip; it then moves to the formation of a group: "it beats being ignored / a carnival of public readings." Writing in such an atmosphere is, as the letter writer twice testifies, easy, but what are the results of such untrammeled production? The last line of the poem, "a bag of cement," gives the problematic answer. Does one want to emphasize the cohesive, constructive possibilities of a bag of cement, or see it as a dead lump too heavy to lift comfortably? In either case, we are beyond the ideology of poetry as organic form. Another letter writer wanted to kill two birds—language writing and poststructuralism—with one stone. He was puzzled that language writing "is so obviously stupid and yet is taken seriously by supposedly reputable scholars. . . . The two seem made for each other—a nonsensical verse explicated by and lionized by a criticism of gibberish."[11]

But in fact such a twin juggernaut has not materialized. Most contemporary theory, if it comes into contact with poems and novels at all, has seemed more comfortable with nineteenth-century works than with contemporary writing. And when critics with a more literary bent have dealt with language writing, the outcome has often been similar to the results at *Poets & Writers*. When the issue of *Critical Inquiry* entitled "Politics & Poetic Value" was turned into a book, Jerome McGann's article on language writing required three follow-up pieces, indicating that his claims for the political and aesthetic value of language writing were something of a breach of intellectual decorum, or at least formed an unstable part of a collection which was meant to be inclusive.[12]

For McGann, L=A=N=G=U=A=G=E Writing, as he referred to it, was not just a new experimentalism. Rather, it represented a critique of U.S. imperialism, and beyond that of capitalism itself. McGann offered qualifications as to the unity of such a project, but they paled in the glare of so politicized a goal. McGann read L=A=N=G=U=A=G=E Writing, not as another voice added to a plural choir, but as a repudiation of the ways of reading and writing poetry that underlay the plurality.

While McGann placed the L=A=N=G=U=A=G=E project in a large social context, he did not attach much importance to its group structure, calling it a "loose collective enterprise" (253). He focused on the particularity of each reader and each reading, stating that the anti- and non-narrative modes used in L=A=N=G=U=A=G=E Writing cause the "relationships and forms of order [to] . . . shift from reader to reader and from reading to reading. . . . What 'counts' are the multiple perspectives processed through the text along with the reader who takes part in that processing" (267, 271). Responding to McGann, Jed Rasula, a poet and critic closely associated with the language movement, emphasized the primacy of the group. For Rasula, the movement's development of independent networks of criticism and publication was crucial: "It's a singular phenomenon that poets should come to-gether as active *readers* and conceptually adroit *critics* of one another's work. . . . A politics in and a politics of American poetry can never arrive at a full collaboration between writer and reader without the deliberate location and cultivation of an audience" (322).

Charles Altieri's main target was McGann's article, but he attacked Rasula's position as well, doubting the solidarity of the language group. He pointed out that language writers wrote variously and that the work of some could hardly be called political: thus to speak of a common purpose made little sense. He scorned the notion that the liberation of the reader could produce the political effects hailed by McGann. "The reader's sense of his or her interpreta-tive freedom to produce meanings" was "dangerously close to . . . the idea of the free, pleasure-seeking consumer that L=A=N=G=U=A=G=E Writ-ing's doctrines so pompously revile" (306). For Altieri, McGann's "ideals of readerly freedom do little more than curry favor with an audience already committed to the radical gestures of an avant-garde" (307). David Bromwich discounted the whole tempest, remarking magisterially that "there is a prob-lem, perhaps a minor one, about 'the L=A=N=G=U=A=G=E poets,' the heroes [McGann] selects to represent poetic radicalism today. They do not appear, as yet, to write good poems" (327). For Bromwich, language writers were a group like the New Kids on the Block: a jejune promotional entity.

This debate encapsulates a number of the difficulties that language writing is raising as it is comes into contact with the wider spheres of literary studies and theory. Are there political implications to the writing techniques of the movement? Are there literary implications to the movement's cohesiveness? Both of these questions are charged, and they need to be considered together. But defining language writing formally and as a literary movement is not easy.

Even the name is hard to pin down. It is "L=A=N=G=U=A=G=E Writing" for McGann and Altieri. Rasula uses "Language Writing," "emphat-ically deleting the equals signs . . . in order to register [his] disagreement with McGann" (317) over the institutional status of the movement. Bromwich puts the term in quotes: " 'the L=A=N=G=U=A=G=E poets.' " Language writers themselves have been no more united in their terminologies: "lan-guage" is always included, sometimes capitalized, with but mostly without equal signs; the second word is sometimes "poetry," sometimes "writing." There is also "the language school," "the language movement," and the increasingly popular "so-called language writing," which catches the distrust of labels.

Consider the titles of two magazines, which were initially devoted to lan-guage writing: *This* and *L=A=N=G=U=A=G=E*. The first is constructi-vist, the second deconstructive. *This* is a deictic—it points something out;

there has to be somebody doing the pointing: a person using a word, using it specifically, confidently, *this* not *that*. If anything is, *this* is here and now, present and accounted for, but of course the question arises, what is this?

$L=A=N=G=U=A=G=E$, on the other hand, presents a different problem, as anyone who has ever had to type it more than once will understand. The labor of materially producing writing: uppercase L, lowercase equals, uppercase A, lowercase equals, uppercase N, and so on. If the equals signs are focused on, then there seems to be a general functional equivalence, L equals A equals N—a letter is a letter. A Saussurian poetics, perhaps, where sign equals nothing more than its difference from every other sign. Beyond the letters, as in Kaballah, there is the possibility of the universal, all-permissive word, *language*.

Given these two titles, is language writing constructivist, dominated by technique, or disseminative, marginal? It depends on the examples picked.

Two initial anthologies of language writing reflected this unease with identity in their titles: Silliman's *In The American Tree: Language Realism Poetry*, and Douglas Messerli's *"Language" Poetries: An Anthology*.[13] Silliman was using "Realism" to combat the charges of abstraction and obscurity that arose as language writing began gaining public recognition,[14] but in doing so he was commandeering an opposing term. Messerli made two gestures away from group solidarity, putting "language" in quotes (as Zukofsky had done with the "Objectivists") and using the plural "poetries." By the way, the fact that both of these anthologies use "poetry" or "poetries" in their titles valorizes the genre division between prose and poetry that much of the anthologized writing does not respect.

This problem over names mirrors an equally basic problem: how much of a group phenomenon is language writing? And if there is a group, who should be included? Publication makes this latter question charged: Silliman's anthology includes thirty-eight writers; he names seventy-nine more (ending the list with "and others") from whose work an anthology of "absolutely comparable value" could have been gathered.[15] The issue of quality versus community is not so easily settled; but by its insistence Silliman's gesture displays the fragility of formal assertions in the face of social circumstance. If one "writes like" a language writer, then is one a language writer? Conversely, if one "is" a language writer, then is anything one writes language writing? and if one is not writing language writing, then is one a language writer? Can a writer just say she is a language writer? Can the letter writer's poem cited earlier, which she ironically labeled a "Language Poem," be considered one, unironically? Is Jed Rasula, who I called "a poet and critic closely associated with the language movement," a language writer? If he is not, one could hardly deduce that from his writing. (When I asked him if he was one, he said, "Apparently not." To whom is this non-inclusion apparent? He does appear in Silliman's list of seventy-nine.) Is it merely a matter of literary historical happenstance? Is there such a thing as "language writing"? or is there simply "language writing: the literary movement"? And if language writing is primarily a literary movement, how does one defend it against Altieri's point that many language writers write very differently one from another?

Recent anthologies accept these conflicted swirls as facts; often facts to be corrected or transcended. Corrected in the case of the anthology edited by Peter Ganick and Dennis Barone, which explicitly collects work from those writers who did not appear in the Silliman and Messerli anthologies.[16] In his postscript to that edition, Silliman names another series of seventy writers who could easily have been included in the new anthology. In a collection of writing and theory from mostly younger writers in the "language tradition"— another problematic phrase!—published in the magazine *O.blēk*, Peter Gizzi, one of the editors, amplified Silliman's unease with editorial judgment by asserting in his introduction, "This is not an anthology."[17] But relations between literary democracy and editorial choice will never be cordial, short of a permanent hypertext that is free to all. It is one of literary history's ironies that language writing, a movement challenging the social and rhetorical prerogatives of capital, has become a semiproper name that itself bestows a certain amount of cultural capital upon those it covers.

Readings

A neutral description of language writing might attempt to draw a line around a range of writing that was (sometimes) nonreferential, (occasionally) polysyntactic, (at times) programmatic in construction, (often) politically committed, (in places) theoretically inclined, and that enacted a critique of the literary I (in some cases). But a prosecutorial nominalist looking at specific passages might doubt that the term defined anything in particular. Consider the following examples, to which I will add brief comments intended less for thorough elucidation than to suggest the variousness of the writing.

From Rae Armantrout's *Precedence*:

> Postcards
>
> Man in
> the eye clinic
> rubbing his
> eye—

too convincing. Like
memory.

My parents' neighbors' house,
backlit,
at the end of their street.[18]

Armantrout's poem refers directly to the physical world. But matter, epistemology, and psychology jostle tightly. The verisimilitude of the opening
stanza is "too convincing": the man dutifully rubbing his eye makes the poet
find her own clear vision a sham as if the world were an iconographic performance meant to keep the spectators rooted to their places. However, turning
inward to memory, she finds the same facades of certainty and ends the poem
with her own clear but untrustworthy eye-chart. The house her memory provides is seen from her parents' house, which makes it something of an
"I"-chart as well. While the poem contains few words that don't construct
images, images are viewed suspiciously: the neighbors' house is stagily
"backlit"; the whole poem is labeled a "postcard" dutifully sent back to a
distant home. A self exists in this poem: the poet goes places, has parents,
they have neighbors. The sentences, while truncated, are complete, ending
with periods. This poem is not written in a universe all that far removed from
that of the Objectivists; the careful syntax bordering on plain speech and me-
ticulously scored in short lines brings Oppen and Niedecker to mind. But to
consider Armantrout's writing devoted to clarity and plain speech will seem
singularly limited in the light of many of her other poems, where identity and
social location are precisely at issue. Here is the opening of "Attention":

Ventriloquy
is the mother tongue.

Can you colonize rejection
by phrasing your request,

         "Me want?"

Song: "I'm not a baby.
    Wa, Wa, Wa.

    I'm not a baby
    Wa, Wa, Wa.

    I'm crazy
    like you."

The "you"
in the heart of
molecule and ridicule.[19]

This is far from being plain speech, although the bald power struggle between mother and child is plain enough. "Ventriloquy / is the mother tongue" articulates a model of how linguistic subjects are formed through a complex of imitation, control, rebellion that leaves all selves multiple masters and puppets of one another; it is a Lacanian lecture condensed into one memorable sentence. Sound is crucial to this philosophic drama: "Wa, Wa, Wa," the deliberate babytalk that one family member directs against another, shows that regression can be aggression: this is not the pre-Oedipal maternal fullness Kristeva calls the semiotic. But 'mature' language does not fully detach itself from this site of sonic bonding and battle, as the *u*-rhyme between the carefully dispersed trio of "you," "molecule," and "ridicule" demonstrates. To call a molecule "you" is both an emotional obligation and ridiculous.

From David Melnick's *Pcoet*:

ruignging
ther o weigter a owef.

Th. erou tower

    ofv Herm
       on
oswwod paseris

ther apt   I wpsetn
wae
a doz   peoftna   rmoll[20]

Pcoet is in the *zaum* tradition—if an impulse that only wants to create novel objects can be said to have a tradition. Armantrout uses conventional language to express suspicion of the simulacra of memory and the recursive puns of perception; Melnick acts on those suspicions, writing a poem—in terms of its look on the page not that removed from Oppen or Armantrout—in which each group of letters can suggest a mutated or degraded word. The major example of ruin is of course the title, which deftly sabotages the august figure of the poet by inserting a single letter. In the text, is "ruignging" a 'ruined' form of *ruining*? or it can be seen, not so much read, as free from the necessities of language: "ruignging" is almost a palindrome; it's also just a clump of letters confronting over-trained readers dying to make sense at any cost. In a comment on *Pcoet* Melnick disavows communicative intention: "What can such poems do for you? You are a spider strangling in your own web, suffocated by meaning. You ask to be freed by these poems from the intolerable burden of trying to understand."[21]

But what of lines like "tower // ofv / Herm"? Including Melnick's later writing into the reading of *Pcoet* would certainly make the "tower" referential. Herms were pillars with Hermes heads and erections; they served, variously, as boundary markers, priapic cult objects, or garden decor in classic Greece and Rome. Melnick's *Men in Aida* is a homophonic translation of the *Iliad* pressed into the service of a hyperbolic gay comedy. The opening lines are

> Men in Aida, they appeal, eh? A day, O Achilles!
> Allow men in, emery Achaians. All gay ethic, eh?
> Paul asked if tea mousse suck, as Aida, pro, yaps in.
> Here on a Tuesday. 'Hello,' Rhea to cake Eunice in.
> 'Hojo' noisy tap as hideous debt to lay at a bully.
> Ex you, day. Tap wrote a 'D,' a stay. Tenor is Sunday.
> Atreides stain axe and Ron and ideas'll kill you.[22]

Homeric epic is treated both piously and transgressively. In its own words, this writing is a "hideous debt to lay at a bully." Melnick is not merely trying to recreate the 'mood' of the Iliad, as Christopher Logue did a few years back with his expressivist translation-deformation. If it's a question of fetishizing inherited form, why not go all the way? Like Hegel, for whom the spiritual value of the classical languages was manifest even down to their grammatical elements, and like Arnold, for whom Homer represented a natural fact and a primary literary touchstone, Melnick is taking the words of Homer as a sacred given, valuing the actual sound of the Greek over the meaning. And at the same time, he's doing just the opposite: staging a gay orgy on this most platitudinous site. Except that the writing makes for odd porn. The possible to improbable extensions of sense are libidinized and made the occasion of hysterical humor which is not simply funny. Form here is inseparable from issues of social formation. The writing gestures toward the heroic ethos of ancient Greece where homoeroticism was a fact of life while at the same time it is an ultra-camp commentary on the situation of gay culture in contemporary America where homoeroticism is as deviant as the grammar of "Paul asked if tea mousse suck, as Aida, pro, yaps in."

Men in Aida was written a decade later than *Pcoet*, but it can cast echoes of sex and ancient Greece back into the earlier passage that, read in isolation, formally might seem to forbid all ascription of meaning. My larger point here is that consideration of individual career trajectories allows for more complete and complex readings than a generalized formal grid meant to apply to all language writing.

From Bruce Andrews's "I Guess Work the Time Up"

> Zero population growth patting
> rabbit hash undoubtedly inspired
> by the real Negro November 1958's *won't* paternalism
> formerly associate with no compute King Diamonds of Osteopath
> venture Ne Plus Ultra Doze Pigeon Wing get it gets
> renounces Glum Wig Trepidation   First of the one-legged
> two feet square comradorial retard to floor crowded around two
> in the bred from dough can't write my name even
> deluxe accuse affected lungs bed me a forgery   Mrs J
> proverbial two tiny sad sad girl & boy bath rooms roping
> go to material quizzes wheel & deal
> creolization too cerebral mummies
> stringy 4 floors presto Mrs K has two tiny boxes
> meaning "Go War! Go Draft!" to remain
> too dependent on unexpected patternings of things referred to
> (fuck epistemology)
> —Bruce Andrews[23]

Unlike *Pcoet*, this does use words, many words, most of them sites of ideological conflict. Andrews does not intend to resolve this conflict aesthetically. Take "Comradorial retard." The first word encodes "comrade" and alludes to the history of Communism. In America the word still can't be used neutrally. But the suffix spins the word in an entirely different direction: "comradorial" sounds like "ambassadorial," a word more at home in a James novel or a Lowell poem. If "retard" is a noun, which the preceding adjective suggests (the writing does use syntax), then any high tone is immediately squelched: "You retard!" is a mild to vicious insult from grade-school playgrounds, where it's used to hint at genetic damage. A sanguine Marxist might project an optimistic class narrative moving from the lumpen fracture of "Retard!" to the proletarian solidarity of "Comrade!" but the phrase moves in the opposite direction and the larger passage continues to encode conflict. There is no overarching narrative resolution; there is no narrative structure; there are barely any sentences. Phrase jams up against phrase with ferocious pace as if a New York graffiti writer was trying to cover the whole subway system in one night, though here all the trains are in motion. Andrews has no time to finish phrases: his critique of liberalism seems to be "*won't* paternalism," which I hear as the beginning of a sarcastic phrase like *"won't* paternalism save the warring children of the world?" Not that those two words finish off the subject—he continues the critique throughout the twenty-five pages of the poem. The writing is not mimetic, but it does refer quite directly to the historical here and now.

From Steve Benson's "The Town of He":

> For a proper understanding
> the meaning of those words   I read the book
>   myself
>   cut into mouthfuls
>
> . . . .
>
> All proof, all power of disputation seemed to be enclosed
>   in the classical tradition of
>   formal directions for servants
>   We Christians travelled all day without food, eating only
> by night, and then so little as to astonish the earlier men of
> letters and theologians
>
> . . . .
>
>   Sometimes he came home with his head bandaged, and then
> Wendy cooed over him and bathed it in lukewarm water, while he told a
> dazzling tale   They were all convinced that we came
> from heaven   We told them what we could, and from then on,
> on the thirtieth of November, they would raise their arms to
> the sky with a glad cry, then run their hands down the length
> of their examination papers[24]

This, like a significant portion of Benson's work, derives from performance: it was improvised from half-memorized pages of Cabeza de Vaca's journals, *Peter Pan*, Thoreau, Huizinga, and Johnson's *Life of Swift*. When the piece is read entire, the limited range of materials becomes familiar and connections can be seen between actual colonial accounts and the fantasy colonial element in *Peter Pan*; between the rhetorical contentiousness of Abelard and Swift and the absolutist faith of de Vaca; between education and the Lost Boys and natives. But no tight coherence develops, and at any given point the writing might vary between suggestions of extremely complex meanings or enigmatic detritus. "All proof, all power of disputation seemed to be enclosed / in the classical tradition of / formal directions for servants"—if sense is allowed to emerge phrase by phrase and sentence by sentence, and tone is allowed to occur locally and independently, then the sudden semantic bend at the end, rather than constituting an affront to the reader, makes a serious claim as to the coercion involved in pedagogy, equating the formality of logic with the formality of domestic service. A related pattern develops in the following: "and from then on, / on the thirtieth of November, they would raise their arms to the sky with a glad cry, and run their hands down the length / of their examination papers." The switch from colonialist propaganda to university protocol, from native bodies to graded exams, is revealing.

From Ron Silliman's *What:*

>   This woman
>   is seriously allergic to bees. Details
>   like zombies in *Day of the Dead.* Yellow brick
>   facade. Those sentences had 'been about' the letter E.
>   Those painters' silence sealed their fate. At least
>   Rosenberg's coinage, "action painting," caught
>   the heroic individualism, that sense of the romantic that
>   would doom them all. Plastic curtains that mime
>   stained glass. My grandmother, the youngest of 13,
>   was herself raised by a single parent, as was
>   her mother also. Here the houses have all gone stylish,
>   deep mauves of brown with a blue trim. Psyche
>   yourself up for the next line. Watching
>   the traffic 'copter hover over the freeway.
>   The point at which you read each word (the
>   only point there is), two minds share a larger whole.[25]

Where the Benson excerpt moves in and out of complete sentences and the Andrews excerpt avoids them, here each sentence is emphatically complete and conventionally denotative. Silliman has termed this mode of writing the new sentence: it is a mode that describes some of the work of some language writers. For Silliman the straightforward denotative syntax of each sentence is part of a large aesthetic and political project: while there is a repeated sense of contextual disruption between sentences, there is no disruption in the politics, which attempt a unified analysis stretching from minutiae of writing and living as material practices to ideological generalizations. The connections between sentences in places seem arbitrary, as in the beginning, though an associational rhythm often grows quite easy to detect. "Those sentences had 'been about'" triggers "Those painters' silence," which triggers the judgment of action painting (Abstract Expressionism), which triggers the aesthetic presentation of the plastic curtains, which triggers the domestic memories. But reconstituting the writer's associations is something of a stopgap; the basic relation of parts and whole is not so easily resolved. Each sentence is representative of a moment from a different level of society: the question as to whether they combine into a unified project is one that haunts Silliman. Perhaps each sentence is no more than part of a phalanx of dead arbitrariness: "details like zombies from *The Day of the Dead*."

Silliman has been an energetic theorist as well as a writer, and so he would be especially interested in rejecting "those painters' silence," which designates the mystique of the lone, rapt genius to whom analysis and self-consciousness are deadly. This was especially prevalent among the Abstract Expressionists, but a weakened form of this attitude pervaded mainstream poetry circles as language writing was coalescing. There's little sense here— as there is some other places in Silliman's writing[26]—of a critique of the subject: if you want Silliman's opinion of Abstract Expressionism, read what he writes. His hope for communion with the reader, of two minds sharing a larger whole, is also nonironic. The more pages of this book-length poem one reads, the more it resolves into a present-tense autobiography of a politically engaged writer.

From "A Mental Finding," by Kit Robinson:

> The president never explicitly authorizes covert action but signals his approval by means of a mental finding. The public never officially acknowledges this betrayal but indicates its mortification by way of a spiritual loss. The person never actually notices the repetitious layering of experience but circles the planet with a red pencil to convey "error."

> The date
> > June 4, 1989

> > Remember the Beijing Massacre

> > > &

> > Long Live the Students

> The way the world has
> of reversal
> > > The power of absorption
> > > The power of brutal repression

> > (rewrite this later)

> > > Scared teenagers with automatic weapons.[27]

Robinson's work is difficult to pin down to a typical mode. "A Mental Finding" recalls the New York School, especially Ted Berrigan and Frank O'Hara, in the rapidity with which the wit turns serious: the critique of presidential responsibility and media-democracy is light in tone and at the same time rather savage. "Findings" are shadowy enough in American politics: a "mental finding" is a bitter joke encoding political irresponsibility in a tight oxymoron: complete private public authorization. But 'mental findings' also characterize the results of reading poetry.

Unlike the deliberate disruptions of Silliman's new sentences, the sentences in Robinson's prose paragraph are tightly anaphoric: humor and lament are linked in a logical lyrical mourning for the degradation of the public sphere. The serious moments do not avoid wit: "Long Live the Students" gets a grating push from the previous slogan; the reminder to "(rewrite this later)" is only feasible if the author is not being detained by the authorities. But last line shows that the writing can also do without wit.

The following excerpt, from the long poem, "Balance Sheet," plays with abstraction in contexts that recall the workplace:

> In America today, the mainstream has dwindled to a pathetic
> strand of calcified imagery holding the mind in thrall, and the
>   margins are fat
>
> with unlikeliness. Weeks go by between sentences, is that what's new
> about them? Remember that variety is an important characteristic
> of the power aisle. Include combinations of large and small items.
> Make sure the signage faces the front entrance. Avoid randomly
>   placed
> stacks or displays. Line everything up in neat, even rows. These
>   cautionary
> trails have been beaten into the bush, and we follow them, not
>   because
> we believe them to be leading anywhere in particular but because
>   they offer
> paths of least resistance into the interior, which generally turns out to be
> someone else's exterior, but that's another story, stopping only to
>   pick
> the burrs from our socks.[28]

Is Robinson giving advice on corporate survival or writing an Art of Poetry? The answer will vary from line to line. If the latter, is it a sarcastic one or not? "Include combinations of large and small items"—what better advice regarding words? There's a nicely sarcastic description of the new sentence[29] in the third line of the excerpt; it also could describe the genesis of this poem.

From "The Wide Road," a collaborative work by Lyn Hejinian and Carla Harryman:

> Paranoia results from that old religious preoccupation with the smallest detail and with similarities. And travelling as we are, we can't indulge in self-portraiture, even when we are stark naked. In fact, much of the time we exceed the perfect differences between you and us, since they are the details demarcating the biological depths and social heights, part history and part isolation. Meanwhile, we incite ourselves to introspect and expect—is this love? is this theory?—we are not experts of postponement.

> > Our head is round, such is life
> > have we not hatched it?

> "We can't get that poem out of our head," we said. We are slaves of environment.

> He is standing behind and above us on the slope and puts his arms around us, passing his fingers over our breasts and reaching between our legs.

> From this elevation, or apparent elevation, we have a remarkable look over a high gray fence into the yard where outdated statuary is stored at the face of an eroded cosmonaut and at 17 arms and forefingers of Lenin.
>   . . . .

> > We come closer to facing
> > the frightening malleability
> > of gender.[30]

The main character or characters—the "we"—in this on-going collaboration is engaged on a picaresque journey through a landscape where gender is as discussable and inescapable as the weather. Narrative is entertained provisionally, though it often seems subservient to philosophy. The critique of religious systems in the opening sentence appears to be a larger frame than the descriptive fact that the narrators are traveling naked. The narrative seems to have as much plausibility as the represented plural self in the piece has physical validity. Here, the "we" accurately reflects the fact that two writers are writing; at the same time the constructed quality of the represented self is impossible to ignore when the man passes his fingers over "our" breasts and reaches between "our" legs. The cult of Lenin's personality is effectively critiqued by citing the 17 phallic pointers toward inevitable historic progress; but the body of the narrator is also problematic: how many breasts and legs are being caressed?

Insofar as critical battles are being fought over the issue of how language writing affects the reader, and what the political consequences are, I think the results will remain equivocal: to the extent that specific work is actually *read*, and not just referred to. These examples—and I could have chosen a number of other equally disparate ones—in turns use conventional syntax or not; use words or not; are mimetic or not; use the first person or not. In some cases, there is also quite a bit of variety within a single writer's work.

Fusing Reading and Writing

So, yes, this various writing needs to be read variously, and there are complex literary effects and antecedents in play at all points. Nevertheless, I want to oppose this empirical point in two ways, and to propose that language writing is best understood as a group phenomenon, and that it is one whose primary tendency is to do away with the reader as a separable category. I realize that this last idea makes a problematic slogan. If language writing wants to do with the reader, why wouldn't readers want to do away with language writing? Bromwich's reaction would seem inevitable: poems not addressed to a reader would have a hard time being "very good," judged by the readerly criteria presumably employed.

On the other hand, in theory-oriented circles, this could seem like little more than a call for Barthes' writerly text, and at first glance, it is somewhat similar. Barthes' proposals, at the beginning of *S/Z*, for a writing that would "make the reader no longer a consumer, but a producer of the text"[31] seems quite close what is often called for by language writers and what often happens with language writing. But the position of a reader 'producing' a reading of a text that is already before her eyes is closer to that of a graffiti writer confronting a poster than it is to a reader turning writer and writing a new text. And while, technically, *S/Z* is a new, written text, it is still a polyvalent gloss on classic text, *Sarrasine*. In practice, there are readers of readerly texts and readers of writerly texts. The readings may differ, but it is only in a metaphorical sense that *S/Z* is a rewriting of *Sarrasine*. Even the *of* in "a rewriting of *Sarrasine*" makes my point.[32]

To give a better sense of what I mean by doing away with the reader as a separable category, let me give a brief, subjective narrative of one technique of language writing. The technique itself is not terribly significant, but it furnishes a conveniently compact model of the way language writing tends to make the borders between writing and reading especially fluid.

"Instead of ant wort I saw brat guts." This line is the epigraph to *In The American Tree*. In a canonical literary history, one addressed to a judging reader, such a phrase would make quite a limited aesthetic object. But as I am interested in non-canonical or anti-canonical sets of literary narratives where literary history is created by writers, I'll give the circumstances of the birth of this line.

Kit Robinson, Steve Benson and I began a writing project almost as soon as we met in San Francisco in 1976. One of us would read from whatever books were handy and two of us would type. These roles would rotate; occasionally, there would be two readers reading simultaneously to one typist. The reader would switch books whenever he felt like it, and jump around within whatever book was open at the time. Truman Capote's slam at Kerouac's work—that this was typing, not writing—would have been even truer here, though none of us could type as fast as Kerouac, who apparently was a terrific typist, an ability which undoubtedly helped give his writing its enviable fluidity.

This was not automatic writing; automatic listening would be more like it. There was no question of keeping up with the stream of spoken words; one could attempt to attend to them or not. If I felt no spark of imagination I would type at or toward the next batch of them I heard, though the rates of speed of spoken syllable versus typed letter were so disparate that by the time a phrase such as "For the purposes of this paper, I will assume a familiarity with Foucault's critique of the notion of the author as an individual" was read[33] I might have managed to type "For the purposes of paper." At that point, I may have started to hear a tone in the typed phrase I wanted to pursue. I can have a sickened fond loathing longing for sentences that start with "For": they remind me of an ersatz biblical loftiness, however many degrees removed from that I remain. So I might continue on my own unmarked track and write, "For the purposes of paper are not the purposes of words alone." By this time, the reader-as-pronouncer might be in the midst of pronouncing "or take the shuttle bus from Gare du Nord with poets, novelists, editors, bookstore owners, Lacanian psychoanalysts, and spend the day."[34] That would certainly come in handy, for instance in producing: "For the purposes of paper are not the purposes of words alone but of poets and novelists, Lacanian psychoanalysts, bookstore owners, and other figures of speech bartering their thought balloons for a bronzed handle on the deeper cellars of the city's statuesque psyche."

We did this for a few months, generating many pages which we worked on, picked through, or mostly filed away. A few lines show up in a few pieces of Robinson's *Down and Back*, Benson's *As Is*, and my *7 Works*. "Instead of ant wort I saw brat guts" begins my book, although in fact Robinson heard/typed/wrote it. It's in 'his voice.'

I don't want to make claims for this process as representative of language writing; no published work that I know of has been written using this method. But I want the extremity of this process, where reading and writing, hearing and producing words were so jammed together, to emblematize an important collaborative element of the beginnings of the language movement. In the above description, I notice that the conventional positions of (modernist) literary competence are reversed: instead of the writer being powerful and the reader struggling to catch up, having to read Dante's Italian, Ovid's Latin, and the Elizabethans in their entirety to be able to read "The Waste Land," in the brat guts literary regime, the reader—or, to avoid confusion, the pronouncer—is the active one and the writer, the typist, the swamped receiver, is reactive, is second in the chain of command, which becomes a chain of suggestion.

Collaborations form a significant portion of published language writing, and beyond these there is an pervasive environment of collaboration on the formal level, with writers often initiating parallel projects; but in this the movement does not differ from, say, the New York School, especially the second generation, or the Surrealists. Much more significant is the blending together of the roles of reader, writer, poet, critic, theorist, publisher and reviewer. Many language writers can write as intellectuals, not just poets; and many poems trespass, in various seemly to unseemly ways, on the territory conventionally reserved for criticism. (E.g., Armantrout's self-critique, "Man in / the eye clinic / rubbing his / eye—// too convincing"; Andrews' brusque, but philosophical dismissal, "fuck epistemology"; Silliman's critique of Action Painting.) And the self-generated reading, publication, and reviewing venues that Rasula mentions were crucial in not allowing separated poetic or critical decorums to develop. The reviews in $L=A=N=G=U=A=G=E$ magazine were notorious for only quoting, or for chopping up, or for otherwise refusing to differentiate themselves from, the books under review, declining all authoritative, critical distance. The books 'under review' were not so much read, as rewritten—in a far more literal sense than happens with *S/Z*. The Talks Series was an effort in this direction, with some talks as much group performance pieces as presentations by an individual to a group.

When I gave my talk "The First Person,"[35] Barrett Watten in the audience scribbled furiously through most of it. He wasn't taking notes on my unsynthesized compendium of first person writing positions, he was using the words I was speaking to write with: one can read shards of the talk in his poem "Statistics" in *1–10*:[36]

> But "pyramids, tombs, chariots of 'personal experience'" want confusion of "schoolboy torn in half" in an odd, "theoretical" way. Transcription stood, the "8-year-old sentient gone": "speaking" twelve feet from the water, its "audience" on the rock. He wanted "baleful 'all-knowing' distance" out of this borrowed substance "often more personal than he." . . . . "Let me in" pushed between "to have intelligibility" hopeless repetition "which takes you away."

If Watten took some of his vocabulary from my talk, one of the passages I quoted in that talk was from my book *a.k.a.*,[37] which owed a great part of its formal instigation to his prose piece, "City Fields."[38] Ron Silliman would later label such collaged sentences, "new sentences." The passage from *a.k.a* that I quoted in my talk and that Watten rewrote included these sentences:

> Everybody gets a biography. Pinholes effect the maximum registration. Vocabularies set up camp on a blurred, running, bloody map. Now they write the lyrics out so I'll know what the song is talking about. Schoolboy torn in half by book. An italicized *i* staggers down the street, making its demands known to the traffic. . . . Two thousand year old empire in eight year old brain.

Looking my sentences now through the lens of Watten's poem, I read a reiterated drama of education: "Schoolboy torn in half by book. Two thousand year old empire [i.e., Latin, etc.] in eight year old brain." Maps are bloody, and italicized *i*'s for whom educational procedures are a mocking ritual of exclusion end up talking to the traffic. I seem to be anxiously regarding a narrative in which language becomes instrumentalized: first they sing, but later "they write the lyrics out," and songs talk. The last sentence in Watten's poem ("Let me in" pushed between "to have intelligibility" hopeless repetition "which takes you away") calls up related questions of acceptance, mastery, bureaucratization, history, and death, all of which are present and unresolved in the narrative of reaching maturity in language.

If the brat guts aesthetic is taken to represent the infant stage of writing—somewhere between Lacan's imaginary and symbolic stages with the baby looking in the mirror of the word stream and lisping his own non-reflective attempts at the typewriter—and if writing like my *a.k.a.* and Watten's "Statistics" can represent going to school (in however conflicted a way), then the 'developmental level' of the following example of collaborative language writing will instantly be grasped as 'more advanced'—possibly even as 'adult'. I am evoking this narrative of maturity sardonically because it's not clear if an 'adult'—i.e., normalized—language writing would be language writing at all.[39] But an address to a wide, impersonal audience can be clearly perceived in the following:

AESTHETIC TENDENCY AND THE POLITICS OF POETRY: A MANIFESTO

For anyone who has been following American poetry over the last decade, it is evident that there has been an intense and contradictory response— from enthusiasm and imitation to dismissal and distortion—to our work. "Our work," in this instance, is part of a body of writing, predominantly poetry, in what might be called the experimental or avant-garde tradition. Its history, while not nearly so canonized as the earlier example, say, of Surrealism, has been generally acknowledged along these lines: around 1970, a number of writers, following the work of such experimenters as Gertrude Stein and Louis Zukofsky, began writing in ways that questioned the norms of persona-centered, "expressive," poetry. (261)

This is from an article Benson, Harryman, Hejinian, Silliman, Watten, and I wrote for *Social Text* in 1988.[40] The opening now seems to me somewhat problematic in revealing ways. The question of imitation and distortion seems odd. In the brat guts aesthetic, certainly, there is nothing but distortive imitation—-no originary clarity to be received accurately. The narrative of the avant-garde tradition presupposes a sequence of literary groups, but in our case, even though group structure was a crucial given, a set group identity was not. In writing the article, we had great trouble with the words *we* and *our*. We wanted *we* to apply locally in the article; but *our* was to indicate language writing as a whole: "In terms of its reception "our work" can mean the writing of up to several dozen writers who have been identified as part of an aesthetic tendency whose definition is not a matter of doctrine but of over-lapping affinities. Here, *we* stands for a consensus arrived at for the purposes of this article among six of its members on the West Coast" (261).

Our use of the word *our* doesn't match our use of *we*. We could not nar-rativize the entire, amorphously defined group and simultaneously embody the subject of such a narrative. We six authors were not interested in making a case for our own writing, but of making three claims for the value of language writing as a whole: 1) that it is a group phenomenon; 2) that language writing not only critiques the norms of voice and self but addresses political and epistemological spaces that voice- and self-poems do not; and 3) that theory can be useful for this.

Why didn't we simply name this body of writing? While we were clearly dealing with the subject of language writing, we avoided that name. Near the end of the article we wrote, "While we are flagrantly writing this article as a group, the perceptive reader will already have noticed that until this point neither the "Language School" nor "Language Poetry" has been named. This is no accident" (272–73). The literary dynamics here are as follows: internally, group structure is crucial: language writing is the activity that blurs the distinction between reader and writer, poet and critic; externally, group identity is disavowed: given the deep disinterest in poetics of identity, the creation of literary labels would hardly be desirable.

From the outside, the process of identification was simpler. Although we had entitled the piece for *Social Text* "Aesthetic Tendency and the Politics of Poetry," when it was published the editors added the designation "A Manifesto." Perhaps their perceptions were colored by the fact that we had mentioned the Surrealists as a prior avant-garde movement. But the Surrealists, in addition to their definite name, had an organization where membership was a matter of charged definition. Along with this barrier between the group and the world went a narrative of apocalyptic literary-social change, which was also crucial for Breton's definition of his movement: "I believe in the future resolution of these two states, dream and reality, which are seemingly so contradictory, into a kind of absolute reality, a *surreality*, if one may so speak."[41]

On the other hand, in writing our piece, the six of us had no desire for a rigorously structured and self-defined group and no such absolutist designs on the future. For us, the avant-garde was a "tradition" in which we situated "our work"; we also placed that writing in or near to the same field as postmodern theory. In these circumstances, a manifesto hardly seems a feasible, let alone a desirable, genre, given the separation that a manifesto inevitably implies between advanced writers and benighted readers.

Such a separation is what the movement wants to overturn. A public is addressed not as readers but as writers. The formalisms and disruptions of convention that variously mark language writing function to remind readers that they are also producers and not just receivers of language.

Of course, all readers of all poems use language. But where many poems aspire to the finality of aesthetic completion, language writing represents a struggle, not to make inescapable sense ("Perhaps I've been struggling too hard over the years to make my poems make sense," as the letter writer put it), but to unmake just such final sense, and to allow room for further efforts from the readers/writers. "To allow room for further efforts" feels too pat. "To construct room for further efforts" is better—such openings can be hard to open and to keep open. The conventional reproach, "I could do that," should actually be taken as a good sign, as a response a writer might seek rather than fear.[42] A better sign might be, "I could do something a bit different than that."

Bromwich's arch conclusion—"They do not appear, as yet, to write good poems"—contains a similar reproach, with the "as yet," implying a narrative of aesthetic maturity: perhaps one day they *will* write good poems—what I'm calling closed poems that can only be read. But if my picture of language writing is valid, the various trajectories of the writers will bypass Bromwich's narrative. His assumptions of unchanging literary quality will be irrelevant to the struggles for effective, open interaction among users of language. After all, history, even literary history, teaches that change occurs. Denham and Waller used to be better than Shakespeare; Longfellow better than Whitman. In the latter case, it wasn't even close.

There are limited temporal spans to groups: individual writing careers tend to get separated out. The language movement has generated a considerable body of poems, prose, and writing which falls somewhere in the middle, and these writings tend to go their own ways as they circulate. Writers who weren't part of the original group are now often considered language writers. The challenges and invitations this work presents are also perceptible to readers who may not know anything about language writing as a category.

If we are to escape a future where already written poems furnish the models on which explication, criticism, theory work their isolate wiles, then we need to validate the irate letter writer stabbing pen onto page, and, all irony aside, producing something for which there is no prior authorization, as much as we appreciate the exuberant marginalia of a Barthes or the frosty agonies of a de Man in his stony aporetic literary garden. Language writing can be placed in a sequence including modernism, the Surrealists, the Objectivists, Black Mountain, the New York School, but while it can be subsumed within a readerly literary history, it holds out the possibility for new social possibilities for writers who might find literary history less burdensome, more useful.

THREE

Here and Now on Paper: The Avant-garde Particulars of Robert Grenier

> "I'm new, said she, I don't think you'll find my card here . . . I'm new, said the oval moon. . . . I'm new, said the quartz crystal. . . . I'm new, said the mist rising from the duck pond. . . . I'm new, says the great dynamo."
> —William Carlos Williams, *The Great American Novel*

Origins

The opening issue of *This* magazine was as much of an originary moment as language writing can be said to have. As one way of considering the relations of individual writer and group, I want to outline the progress of Robert Grenier's career from his founding of the magazine with Barrett Watten in 1971 to his idiosyncratic recent work (as of 1995), which consists in large part of photocopied holograph pages and drawings. In one sense, it is a truism to say that the medium in which this trajectory has its meaning is literary—most of what Grenier has written is easily identifiable as poetry; his critical pieces and talks are about poetry; and his nontypographic work has been published in venues that frame it as poetry. This latter part of his work is not very anomalous anyway: literary history has a small but operant category for concrete poetry, and for drawn and shaped poems from those of Herbert to Apollinaire's *Calligrammes* to Philip Whalen's work in *On Bear's Head*, not to mention Eastern calligraphic traditions; one can add recent critical work by Susan Howe and Marta Werner where the use of space in Emily Dickinson's holographs is read as intentionally significant.[1] But to place Grenier's latest work unproblematically in literary history also distorts it since it seems to manifest a desire to escape all literary historical grids and to make direct contact with the world via pen and paper. His writing has become intensely personal and it does not seem constructed to represent anything other than itself. But though his allegiance to a group identity such as language writing is now decidedly tepid, I find a conflict in his work that occurs to some extent in the work of various other language writers. At a basic level, this conflict is between the autonomous activity of writing and the structures of meaning—letters, words, lines, sentences, genres—that cannot begin to exist without becoming entangled in the widest literary historical mediations.

Writing as an activity—pen marking paper, fingers tapping keyboard—is not synonymous with writing as a product, i.e., a poem or a body of work, even though it is via the contingency of activity that complete structures come to exist. Grenier's later scrawls will bring us up close to this elemental trouble, but from a distance the lack of synonymy is hardly revelatory. Process versus product is an old aesthetic battle; Allen Ginsberg is not Richard Wilbur, nor is Pollock Mondrian. The administered dioramas of literary history contain scenes that on a gross scale can be read clearly enough, so that we can watch revolutionaries battling conservatives and fighting against genres and the genres themselves flourishing, fading, and mutating. But even if we could ignore the hierarchical procedures that underlie the construction of histories, encyclopedias, and canons, it would be difficult to dispel a blander source of hypnotic clarity: chronology. Literary causality and literary justice can be argued at whatever length: but whether or not *Emma* gave birth, in any sense, to *Ulysses*, Joyce comes after Austen in the history of the novel. Teleology, with its soothing sense of inevitability and finality, can creep into any chronicle.

For Paul de Man literary progress is ineffable; he defines it as a permanent aporia that surfaces repeatedly as great works try to come into contact with the nonliterary present.[2] For Theodor Adorno it is quite specific; he defines it via tendentious examples, calling Schoenberg progressive, Stravinsky reactionary.[3] But for a writer the problem is more intimate and immediate. A short poem by Basil Bunting provides a metaphoric narrative of the conflict, beginning with the creative impulse describing itself euphorically but almost instantly ending in the disgust of closure:

> molten pool, incandescent spilth of
> deep cauldrons—and brighter nothing is—
> cast and cold, your blazes extinct and
> no turmoil nor peril left you,
> rusty ingot, bleak paralysed blob![4]

The disgust couldn't have been greater than the pleasure the finished blob afforded, however, since the poem was one of the few to survive Bunting's notoriously rigorous self-editorializing glare. Notions of progress look even less likely from the vantage of the blank page or screen, where it is a matter of a yet-to-be-written poem and a yet-to-be-defined literariness—of making a career and entering and changing literary history. The singularity of each new word is simultaneously involved with its own compositional context and with the tactical battles of literary history: the future is up for grabs (and in some cases the past as well). Unsecured area is being fought over: reviewers, critics, readers, students, professors, publishers, owners of book stores, not to mention the writer's own practice.

Venues as well as poems are sites of such struggles. In 1971 Grenier and Watten began the magazine *This*, the first self-conscious journal of what would become known as language writing. The name and character of the movement were uninvented at the time, nor were many of the future partici-pants in touch yet, but the magazine was clearly motivated by a sense of literary progress. The first issue contained a particular phrase of Grenier's, "I HATE SPEECH," that, in hindsight, was an important literary gesture: it was singled out by Ron Silliman ten years later in his introduction to the first anthology of language writing, *In The American Tree*, as "announc[ing] a breach—and a new moment in American writing,"[5] although the "breach" now seems too dramatic. At the time there were many writers, involved in different social formations and providing various formal models, from which language writing would arise. A short list would include figures associated with Black Mountain, the New York School, the San Francisco Renaissance: Charles Olson, Frank O'Hara and Jack Spicer, each of whom had recently died but whose work was still appearing; Robert Creeley, Robert Duncan, Larry Eigner; the aleatory work of Jackson Mac Low and John Cage; John Ashbery, Ted Berrigan, Alice Notley, Clark Coolidge, Bernadette Mayer, and Ron Padgett; Tom Raworth, David Bromige, and Michael Palmer.[6] The Ob-jectivists were still active and were in fact a much stronger presence than they had been in prior decades: George Oppen had just won the Pulitzer Prize and Louis Zukofsky was in the process of finishing *"A."* (He would give *"A"*-22 its first and as far as I know its only reading at Franconia College at Grenier's invitation in 1972.) Lorine Niedecker's work was beginning to circulate. Some high modernists were resurfacing: Laura Riding's *Selected Poems* had just been reissued more or less simultaneously with Laura Riding Jackson's *The Telling*, which bade poetry an emphatic farewell; Pound was alive and—who knew?—might yet be finishing *The Cantos*. William Carlos Williams, especially the early work, Mina Loy, and Gertrude Stein were among those appearing for the first time for most readers: in *This* 1 Grenier reviews her republished *Lectures in America*. It would be relatively easy to pick out from the work of these writers a great deal of writing that would match if not surpass that of the language writers in disjunction, nonsyntacticalness, and nonreferentiality.

Compared to the range of formal possibilities and social groupings and postures this partial list includes, the work and literary information in *This* 1 was quite limited. But "I HATE SPEECH" and Grenier's criticism in general were important in its positing of literary space. It established, at least in embryonic form, a way of connecting private reading and writing desires with some sense of public consequence and thus with a future. All the above writers could conceivably be used, not simply read.

One could see, without reading any of the words in the issue, that *This* 1 issued a double appeal to fresh beginnings and revered ancestors. The cover displayed drawings by Grenier's very young daughter Amy done at the stage when signification was just beginning to emerge from marks on paper (i.e., when big circles first mean heads and two smaller circles with centered dots mean eyes). Balancing this originary gesture, inside were photos of the masters: one of Charles Olson, who had died the previous year, and one shot from street level of the very old Pound sitting in a chair in a second-story apartment facing Olga Rudge, who was staring out the window. While the Olson photos were captioned and attributed, the photo of Pound and Rudge was not, as if to emphasize a casual connectedness: one might simply go to Venice and—quite outside the tortuous routines of institutional criticism—encounter Pound, at least from a distance.

The issue's simultaneous claim to originariness, a tradition, and a productive future follows the basic pattern of Pound's, Zukofsky's, and Olson's manifestos. Schematically: in the name of the true poetic ancestor one dismisses the false (because outmoded) writing of the present to clear the way for the future. Recall Zukofsky's definition of "an objective" as "*Desire for what is objectively perfect, inextricably the direction of historic and contemporary particulars.*" The definition covers both poetry and history. But while Zukofsky's Marxism might specify an inevitable historical teleology, in poetry perfect consonance with historical momentum is rare; most importantly, all else is, apparently, dismissible: "Omission of names is prompted by the historical method of the Chinese sage who wrote, 'Then for nine reigns there was no literary production.' None at all; because there was neither consciousness of the 'objectively perfect' nor an interest in clear or vital particulars."[7] Pound was Zukofsky's source for the "Chinese sage" (and certainly the model of such 'sage' literary aggression).[8]

The basic tension of this modernist gesture has been exacerbated by the debate over multiculturalism. It is one thing if Zukofsky is seen as an outsider, a son of Yiddish-speaking immigrants; but if he is seen as placing himself at the cutting edge, of history and of aesthetics, then his dismissal of all other writing will rankle those who see themselves as outsiders. The flames of this debate can be encapsulated by the comment of Saul Bellow (not the Jewish novelist but the Nobel laureate): "Where is the Tolstoy of the Zulus?" The question is absurd, really, as it ignores the dependence of individual achievement on social conditions—"Where is the Werner von Braun of the Mennonites?" The notion of literary progress can never distance itself completely from this absurdity: to posit a gap between "objectively perfect" (perfectly progressive) literature and all other writing that is to be denied the status of literature is to designate the winner of the race while denying that there are other contestants. Though Zukofsky's dismissing all other literature is something like a mirror image of Bellow's gesture, the positions from which the gestures are made should be kept in mind. Bellow's remark is the classic condescension of the threatened gatekeeper.

The poetry in the first issue of *This* does not now seem very close to "objectively perfect," but it was not the key matter; while there was work by four writers who would later be part of *In the American Tree*, the bulk of the poetry was by Robert Creeley, Robert Kelly, Ken Irby, Anne Waldman, Anselm Hollo, and Tom Clark—New American and second-generation New York School poets. Ten years down the road, Clark would attack language writing assiduously, even though in the interim he himself would have written poems that could be called 'language-esque' (for instance, "The Great Song," in his New York School anthology *All Stars*).[9] Strict registration of formal features is rarely a strong factor in poetry wars. Claims on literary direction and location are what is notable.

The writing that gave the issue a forward trajectory and thus a center of gravity was Grenier's critical prose: celebratory, intimate responses to Stein's *Lectures in America*, and to Creeley's *Pieces* and his essays, *A Quick Graph*; and one more general piece entitled "On Speech." Grenier wanted the distinction between poetry and criticism abolished; "in the work that matters, comment is finished, there will have to be no essential difference between criticism and poems"—though as the sentence continues the essentiality of poetry glides back in—"if for no other reason than that poems are going to be so real that nobody will want to read 'about' anything." The Stein piece was in fact all quotations except for a final paragraph in which Grenier affirmed that her critical writing was fully realized as poetry. (The critical piece that was all quotation would later become an almost standard form in $L=A=N=G=U=A=G=E$ magazine. Zukofsky's book-length critical collage *Bottom: On Shakespeare* was one precursor; in a different context, Walter Benjamin had called for such a practice in the thirties.) The one reservation Grenier had about Creeley's essays was that in places they were only expository and referential: "Despite the intelligence and care with which each sentence is written . . . typically it means something apart from the fact of its own existence."[10]

The aim may have been a self-presence of poems such that criticism would become obsolete, but the most influential moments in *This* 1 were criticism, especially the phrase "I HATE SPEECH," thanks in part to Silliman's later use of it. The differences between the way Silliman read the phrase and the context in which Grenier wrote it are instructive. For Silliman the temporal expanse of American writing was the obvious medium in which Grenier's gesture acted as it called into question Olson's emphasis on the page as a vocal score and more directly attacked confessional poetry of the fifties and sixties that at the time was modulating into the dominant form of the poetry workshop first-person lyric. Silliman was aware that there were contradictions here. The workshop lyric could, like Projective verse, claim lineage from Pound and Williams, since modernist aesthetics was, to a significant degree, speech-based: Pound proselytizing in favor of directness, commanding the writer to write only what, "in the stress of some emotion, [you] could actually say"; Williams claiming that he took his language "out of the mouths of Polish mothers."[11] But such contradictions occurred in a large social and historical background; on the local level, Silliman could read Grenier's phrase as a historicized call to focus on textuality.[12]

But if we look beyond that one phrase, Grenier's essay was less involved with tactical positioning and bore a more tangled, less historicized burden. It begins: "It isn't the spoken any more than the written, now, that's the progression from Williams, what now I want, at least, is the word way back in the head that is the thought or feeling forming out of the 'vast' silence/noise of consciousness experiencing the world **all the time**." To an extent, this evocation of high modernism and a pre-verbal state replicated the visual dyad of photos of the masters and child's drawings I mentioned previously. Literary progress—"the progression from Williams"—was the overriding goal, but the locus of activity was also personal: the originary, omnitemporal space "way back in the head." As a further twist this call was framed as an echo of modernist gestures: where Williams had written: "*All* sonnets mean the same thing,"[13] Grenier wrote: "**To me, all speeches say the same thing**, or: why not exaggerate, as Williams did, for our time proclaim an abhorrence of 'speech' designed as was his castigation of 'the sonnet' to rid us, as creators of the world, from reiteration of the past dragged on in formal habit. I HATE SPEECH." This repetition of a prior originary act in the name of novelty is similar to Williams's destroying and re-creating the world in the opening prose of *Spring and All*: Grenier wanted to join in the creation of an already created world. (All originary gestures also "say the same thing.") His attack reenacted Williams's attack, with the workshop voice poem as the target rather than the genteel sonnet; and by using capitals, he aligned himself with Pound and Olson, eschewing the normative prose in which Eliot, Richards, and all the others kept critical accounts separate from poetry. To use caps is to be an outsider; one is not keeping track of literary history; one is making it (new), like

Pound, like Williams, like Stein, like Zukofsky, like Olson, like Creeley. The aim is simultaneously toward a lineage and a singular point of openness.

For Grenier, Creeley's then-new *Pieces* defined that point. He began his essay on it with the assertion that " 'PROJECTIVE VERSE' IS **PIECES** ON." That is, *Pieces* was the next valid literary step forward ("ON") in the chain that Olson called for when he wrote, "ONE PERCEPTION MUST IMME-DIATELY AND DIRECTLY LEAD TO A FURTHER PERCEPTION."[14] Olson may have been referring to moments of writerly consciousness, but his subsequent practice strongly suggested that "PERCEPTION" could also be read as "FORMAL BREAKTHROUGH." This would not be "FORMAL ICONOCLASM," however; " 'PROJECTIVE VERSE' IS **PIECES** ON" pos-ited a specific direction for the future of poetry. It is not a matter of simply trying out panoplies of new techniques: they were as useless as the outmoded forms of the past. Grenier asked: "What can be done. Evidently not more sonnets, and not force 'experiment.' " The direction of literary progress in-volved an elementary conflict: it could not go backward, nor could it go ran-domly forward. It was fully embodied in *Pieces*; but it also had to include the tentative variety of the poetry in *This* 1.

Pieces

Pieces is constructed out of pieces that are half-separated, half-united by a single dot; the completion of a poem is marked by three dots. But to speak of completed poems is often too emphatic; the connection between poems is often foregrounded. The three-dot "endings" are often only slightly stronger versions of the single dot "connections." And conversely, each "piece" looks—at least spatially—complete.

> One thing
> done, the
> rest follows.

> Not from not
> but in in.

> Here here
> here. Here . . . (13–14)

If one reads this from something like Creeley's perspective, it is assured, consistent, and open-ended: "One thing" could be read as the line itself, the poem, the construction of the book, or the development of a rhetoric that united, with the utmost economy, an unshakable sense of presence with a quick awareness of textuality. Personal reference has not been banished: most of the words in the above poem derive from the previous poem in *Pieces*, "The Finger," a long semi-narrative meditation on an intense sexual, psychological, and mythic encounter with a woman. "The Finger" begins, "Either in or out of / the mind, a conception / overrides it" and ends "let / me follow." Thus, in "One thing / done," words register both as the barest denotation and as deeply autobiographical at the bodily level. "Follow" implies simple logical connectedness but also the whole panoply of male questing for love, a theme that Creeley investigates in many poems with his rhetoric ranging from the heroic register down through a self-condemned and self-bemused kvetching. "In" is the bare preposition but also implies all the physical and psychic dramas of phenomenology and sexual penetration. The texture of *Pieces* does not proceed from negation; it operates via complete identification with the words such as "in": it is "Not [written] from not, / but [is written from] [with]in in."

Creeley's insistence on self-presence does not preclude awareness of the contingencies of grammar and lineation: the final "Here" is not endstopped and occurs in a line after the third repetition of "here." These competing "heres," pleonastically undercutting their meaning, hint at a basic problem of phenomenology. Not that Creeley shows much engagement with Hegel; nevertheless, Hegel's discussion of verbal reference in *The Phenomenology of Mind* is quite relevant to *Pieces* as well as to Grenier's subsequent writing. In the *Phenomenology*, Hegel easily demolishes any naive hope that writing and the present might coincide. Mockingly suggesting that "a truth cannot lose anything by being written down," Hegel asks the believer in sense-certainty to write down a present fact: when the statement that it is night is read at noon, it turns out to be perfectly false.[15] "This," the tree the believer sees, refers instead, when the viewer turns around, to a house. Those who assert the truth of sense-certainty "say the direct opposite of what they mean . . . the This of sense, which is 'meant', cannot be reached by language."[16] Such a gap is Creeley's central subject; he approaches it wryly, without any sense of impossibility.

> As real as thinking
> wonders created
> by the possibility—
>
> forms. A period
> at the end of a sentence
> which

> began *it was*
> into a present,
> a presence
>
> saying
> something
> as it goes.—(3)

While Creeley can be read as occupying a literary space where personal narratives intersect with elemental demonstrations of deconstruction, all occurring in an elegantly compressed lyricism, his work could also be read as a troubling warning to all subsequent poets who might not be Creeley. In poetic contexts, Hegel's naive believer in sense-certainty is all too often replicated by the naive believer in another poet's work. If the "One thing / done" was *Pieces*, then "the rest," all subsequent writing, would simply "follow,"—in the terms of Zukofsky's manifesto, it would have to be consigned to the category of ephemeral verbal debris that always occurs during those terrible "nine reigns" when "there was no literary production. None at all." Similarly, "in" and "here" would be ultimately dead ends if they were associated too closely with, if not the person, then certainly the career, of Robert Creeley. *Pieces* was exemplary evidence of a fully verbal life advancing to the edge of what had been professionally acceptable.[17] But there had to be room left over: *Pieces* could not fill the literary Here and Now too completely.

Sentences

Sentences, published seven years after *This* 1, was Grenier's answer to the question of *Pieces*. The publication is rare today, so a basic description will be useful: it is a Chinese-style unfolding box covered in dark blue cloth that closes with imitation ivory clasps; inside is a stack of 500 5-by-8 note cards, each with a short poem printed in the center. Since the cards can be shuffled into any order, *Sentences* is an antinarrative object, taking the separations in *Pieces* one step farther. Like *The Cantos*, its title is problematic—is it a singular or a plural noun? Does *Sentences* cohere or do *Sentences* not cohere? But it also mimes the apparatus of a book, and therefore is a book. In its original order the box contained one blank card (frontispiece); a title card: "*SENTENCES* Robert Grenier"; a copyright card; then 500 poems. At the end (that is, on the bottom) was a blank card, then a card with colophon information. While the lack of binding allows for any sequence, Grenier's allegiance is not toward any early version of hypertext. Paper and typeface are specified—"This work was composed on an IBM Selectric Typewriter, using a Courier 72 (10 point) ball. Card stock is 110 lb index white."—implying that the writing has its meaning at its present location and incarnation: "Here" as it were. (This is an implication that will become very much stronger in his latest work.) Each poem is centered on its card; Grenier does not use white space as Susan Howe often does to suggest a wilderness and a feminist antinomian perspective.

I adopt the following order of examples for expository reasons, although any particular order will be false to the form of *Sentences*. Also the nonproportional font used here only approximates Grenier's intentions, and the small amounts of leading in my pages are a poor substitute for the portable sea of white space out of which the following should float:

except the swing bumped by the dog in passing

Why am I sure that this is to be read as beginning with an implied "Nothing moving"? In discussing *Sentences* I will also be exposing the formation of my own reading procedures. Despite its size, this piece is faithful to the principles of verisimilitude and displays a complex perspective: the swing oscillating in the foreground; the dog, prime mover of the scene, just out of sight, *deus absconditus*; even larger and more ineffable, the unspoken still background, the "Nothing moving" that precedes verbalization. Of course, such cosmic scenarios are built of comic materials: dog and swing. Compare Charles Reznikoff's line—"a girder, still itself among the rubbish"—where the physical world becomes the mirror in which one can find, barely but all the more heroically for that, both self and art. For George Oppen that girder was a touchstone: "I think we could live by virtue of [such] lines, these small precise these overwhelming gentle iron lines."[18] Grenier's writing will not offer as secure a world for a self to inhabit. Objectivist iron will often transmogrify into irony.

It will not be easy to contain most of *Sentences* inside a referential frame. Perhaps the following piece can be read as miming the depth of fallen snow:

SNOW

snow covers the slopes covers the slopes

snow covers the slopes covers the slopes

snow covers the slopes covers the slopes

snow covers the slopes covers the slopes

but with the repetitions (between and within the lines) "snow" and "slopes" start to lose their referential bite. The following may be construed as referential:

two trees

But the poem has a more lasting meaning as an object lesson in verbal phenomenology, although whether Hegel would have approved is an open question. Especially when seen in the center of the otherwise blank card "two trees" reveal themselves as, primarily, two words.

Many of the pieces occupy a comic no-man's land between the dictionary and life.

elms back of

vats

Perhaps this records a moment of experience. Maybe there were some elms in back of some vats somewhere, sometime, with a poet in front, recording it. But there is an open-ended comic sense to the poem that only emerges if it is taken as a strictly verbal construction. "Elms" is a literary word *par excellence*: "The sky is leaded with elm boughs" at the end of Canto 106 is the most cathedral-like moment in *The Cantos*[19]; Helen Vendler singles out as exemplary for American poets Elizabeth Bishop's poem about finding an ancestor's painting of an elm.[20] But here the "elms" are back of (with a line break for emphasis) "vats"—the nonliterary sheep of this tiny family of words. Both are four-letter words, but "vats" calls up much that "elms" ignores: industry, waste, lye, Hoffa-like criminal disposal practices, even though its letters nearly evoke the very opposed words "vast" and "vatic."

TWELVE VOWELS

.   breakfast

the sky flurries

Is the field of experience here life or letters? The title is part of the poem: thus it becomes more a goal or set of instructions than a caption: write until there are twelve vowels (counting *y* as a vowel). Title and poem are contemporaneous: if TWELVE were changed to ELEVEN there would be thirteen vowels on the card; THIRTEEN would be correct; so would FOURTEEN. Meanwhile, beneath such calculations: breakfast in a cold world.

The experience that many of the cards evoke is reading. In the following the avaricious reading eye can see itself mirrored.

restless moving to the right

Or, in a more tricky register:

light &

and shade

Of course, contrary to what a first glance might have said, this is neither "light & shade" nor "light and shade." Once the little eye-game is over, "&" and "and" begin to seem expressive. The landscape of print becomes the observed world. Under the glare of its associate "light" the ampersand seems crinkled, toasted, burnt; while the word "shade" shades the more pastoral, cool, quiet, gray "and."

A different registration of pastoral occurs in a number of cards where Grenier tries to transcribe bird song. The tone here feels very much tongue-in-cheek (in beak?), though the desire to equate writing and nature and to write a natural lyric will come to dominate his later work:

A BIRD

who would call

not for me

but for you

in the day

Some of the cards seem taken directly from life. The following may well be a quotation from his daughter, the cover artist for *This* 1.

AMY

don't

mind me

hold the

ballerina

But if this is an event, it is recounted at an angle that obscures any narrative. Whatever has happened or is happening to Amy, her stoic regard for her doll stands out.

AMY

look out
a bridge
water

"AMY" is the title of a number of cards. She seems to function a bit like Dorothy for William Wordsworth as a source of vividness and a link to an originary wilderness within language. Here, at the most elemental level, we have consciousness of perception (or of danger: Look out!), then identification: a bridge; then, sans article, the oceanic perception: water. Such attention is what Zukofsky said his life's work was concerned with: "a case can be made out for the poet giving some of his life to the use of the words *a* and *the*: both of which are weighted with as much epos and historical destiny as one man can perhaps resolve. Those who do not believe this are too sure that the little words mean nothing among so many other words."[21] Zukofsky's sense of his own life depended on such distinctions; after all, his life-epic was called *"A."* Creeley, too, sees his own contingency, his own life and death, mirrored in the substitution of "a" where "the" is expected:

One more day gone,
done, found in
the form of days.

It began, it
ended—was
forward, backward,

slow, fast, a
sun shone . . . (53–54)

—But Grenier's sense of verbal fate in *Sentences* is quirkier, and is spread out to include almost any word:

roams

On a card, this can evoke wan or comic senses of pure motion and minuscule agency. If one is not in the capital (Rome) is one condemned to wander, banished from subjecthood? *Who* roams? *What* roams? What is a "roam"? However, for some, "roams," read in the context of these discursive, critical words, might seem fairly close to a hoax: couldn't any word be substituted?

A sense of social desperation erases the textuality of some of the cards:

what a weird deserted place New Hampshire is

or

that was

awful

no more

attachment

More often the arbitrary is foregrounded:

arriving in potato

Just a joke? Cinderella with a change in vegetable transport? Isn't it also an example of the continual strangeness of all verbal manifestation? Should we say of "MAKE IT NEW" that it always involves "arriving in potato"?

s o m e o l d g u y s w i t h s c y t h e s

One can decode this as "some old guys with scythes" to which one can then attach a narrative of literary value. Not a particularly striking narrative: "some old guys with scythes" is a splotch of scenic description in American folk-speech, perhaps akin to a line from James Wright. More in line with Grenier's macabre comic sense, it could be a phalanx of Father Times or Deaths, with the plural making the ominous authority of The Grim Reaper faintly ridiculous. More pronounced than this is the rhyme: some old *guys* with *scythes,* which can lead one to believe that the rhyme was the engine of the composition. At this point one starts to notice the semidetached letters again: George Bernard Shaw pointed out that "fish" can be spelled "ghoti"; here, "uy" and "y" make the same sound. As a whole, the letters make visible, by distortion, the pattern-recognition that underlies all reading. One can glimpse the process of paragram-formation that pushed Saussure to search endlessly for the names of gods and heroes hidden amid the letters of Latin verse: "omeo" (Where art thou omeo?); "meold," "swiths"—is this olde englisshe?—"yswiths." Mythic

possibilities of an odd textual cast arise: "So me old guy swiths Cythera."
Suddenly a projection of the primal scene: mother is Aphrodite, father is
Saturnus. Such readings are clearly improper.

JOE

JOE

Here, particularly, I can read the formation of my own reading procedures. I
remember being quite boggled by this one. The underlying question when I
spoke with Grenier about these cards was, "Is this one *good enough*? What's
so '*good*' about this one?" These were not exquisite haiku; what was 'good'
often seemed to lie in a much more recalcitrant direction.

Grenier acted out a comic forlorn Romantic scenario: A calling out to B:
"Joe!" Long pause while the human syllable, which is almost animal or mete-
orological in its simplicity, disperses over the snowy fields of the Alps. (Grenier did not say these things—I am adding them now). Call again, since
there's no answer: "Jooooe!" Fled is that signification. Do I wake or sleep, am
I speaking English or lowing? Joe is gone, and what is even sadder, perhaps
never was there in the first place. When we call the world with our noises we
get only the busy signal of our own repetitious words. This is especially true
with names, where signification marks the elemental claim of human connection. The severe classic parallelism of "JOE // JOE" mocks and laments the
broken connection between word and world.

Do I need to say that all of this is very much tongue in cheek? It is *dumb*—
in both a fifth-grade and a Heideggerian sense. Perhaps the feeling of the
futility of such calling out would drive someone to write "I HATE
SPEECH."[22]

These two last paragraphs make clear how great a distance can lie between
what is written and how the writing can be read. The relation of "JOE // JOE"
to my aggressive parody of Romanticism is stretched, to say the very least.
However, I have included this particular poem and my interpretation as a
reminder of just how personal and contingent anyone's entry into the literary
field is. However one gets in, the literary here and now has to remain open
enough to contain all meaning—old and new—or it withers rapidly, at least in
any one reader and writer's experience.

Living Hands

Grenier's involvement with *This* stopped after the fourth issue. In the mid-seventies as the creation of self-managed language writing venues began, Barrett Watten continued editing the magazine and intensified Grenier's interest in a literary future (and thus in literary history). Grenier's own writing went in the direction of the here and now. His latest work is another box, a smaller one, the size that 100 sheets of typing paper used to come in. Its 65 photocopied pages comprise three smaller works that are named in its title: *What I Believe Transpiration/Transpiring Minnesota*.[23] The first section contains some typing;[24] the last two are almost all handwritten, with some drawing; often the page is divided into two with the words on the top half oriented upward and those on the bottom oriented downward. These gestures particularize the moment of utterance even further: rather than the Selectric ball providing the particularity of the poem's print-'voice' as was the case with *Sentences*, now it's the motion of the pen. Such work aims for the asymptote of the Pound ideogrammic tradition, which wants to get away from the fungibility of word and letter.[25] If this is textuality it also tends toward, without reaching it, the idiosyncrasy of the brush stroke.

This work calls into question the boundaries of writing, which of course means it calls into question the boundaries of reading. One prominent aspect of much language theory is the attempt to extend the notion of literariness—the Russian formalist distinction between literary language and ordinary language—into language itself. This makes ordinary literary evaluation problematic; any word ("roams," for instance) or any patch of words ("JOE // JOE") can potentially call for the kind of generative reading normally reserved for highly valued examples of ambiguity or polysemy. The scrawls and overwriting of Grenier's later work put a different spin on this problem of reading: deciphering per se is difficult. Far from finding literariness everywhere, one gets the feeling, trying to decipher a page, of not having gotten to language. The literariness—or at least the special poetic or ontological value or magical potency that Grenier seems to be trying to create—occurs as one moves from this far border of language to the birth of intelligibility.

I'll reproduce two pages. I'll say little about the first (Figure 1) except to note the conflict between the bottom half of the page, which seems to be written under the sign of Williams and ends (as I read it), "I don't dis / integrate, *I go to work*" and the top half, which is "for John Keats" and mentions a "threshhold." These lines (of verse) are made up of words, but they gesture toward an earlier state in which they are simply collections of drawn lines on the far side of the threshold of sense. What lies beyond is an open question: it

Figure 1.

could be the Romantic sublime, or it could be bare evidence of the Here where Grenier's hand moved.[26]

The second page (Figure 2) calls out in a punning way. As I transcribe it the title reads "BOB / MOON RISING"; the date is "Sept 13 / 89"; the dedication is to "*his body* / *Kawishiwi*". Or it could be two titles-with-dedications: "BOB *his body*" and "MOON RISING *Kawishiwi*." However this may be— and I have left out the placement of "MOON" above "RISING" and the large "I" in "RISING"—the text is clear: "*no, please* / not out in the Boat / again tonight / *please*." I'm not sure of the tone Grenier intends—desperate comedy I think—but I am struck by the reference, whether intentional or not, to the stolen-boat episode in Book 1 of *The Prelude*. What terrifies Wordsworth there is the animation of a scene that should be still: as he rows, a second, larger mountaintop emerges from behind a more immediate cliff to monitor him; his oar strokes seem to give the larger mountain motion. Such animation, such contact between writer and world, is what Grenier seems to aim for. But the stolen-boat scenario should remind us that the literary present is not a space that is easily securable. Even as one creates in the present, one is fleeing the larger literary past, which jerks into motion with each stroke of the pen. To avoid this, one would have to abandon words altogether.

I can imagine that to some readers Grenier's recent work might seem a negligible aggression against the idea of literary value. But the value of even the most canonical poems is never a settled fact. The more fully and finally legible a poem is, the less compelling. Grenier's scrawls are nothing if not poems, and as such they dramatize in a particularly problematic way the tautological narrative by which the "living hand" of the contingent author becomes imbued, after the fact, with eternal potency. The canonical status of *Ulysses* makes Joyce's earlier notebooks precious. But one can turn the lens the other way round and look at the particular piece of paper one is writing on; from such a vantage literary history can also seem a baleful reification, the largest collection of minatory crags, old hats and rusty ingots, bleak and paralyzed.

Outside of eternity, Grenier's writing has called forth a variety of responses within the language community. One of the most involved was that of his former co-editor, Watten, who ended a review in 1978 with the provocative remark that *Sentences* contained no sentences and that "there is certainly much more to be done, starting with—writing in sentences."[27] This was more or less coterminous with the beginning of new sentence writing, which I will discuss in the next chapter. This admonition to pay attention to the social context of words could mark the conclusion to this chapter.

However, to critique the unmediated junction between nature and language

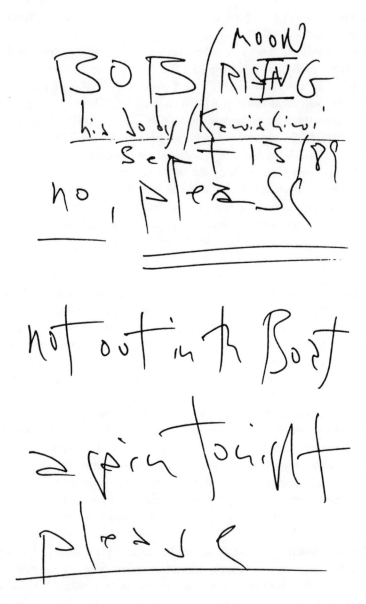

Figure 2.

that Grenier is trying to arrange, and in a kind of critical homage to the humor with which he stages the confrontation, I want to conclude with another passage from *The Prelude*. It is the moment of crossing the Alps, when Wordsworth sees the mountains as the

> workings of one mind, the features
> Of the same face, blossoms upon one tree,
> Characters of the great Apocalypse,
> The types and symbols of Eternity,
> Of first and last, and midst, and without end.[28]

Legibility, the automatized perspicuity that familiarity with letters and literary history provides, can mask important aspects of writing. One can always miss the event of sense, in much the same way as Wordsworth missed the experiential moment of crossing the Alps. Verbal sense is signification and sonic and visual perception at once; to bring the paradox of this union into sharper focus I will quote this passage at closer range in order to grasp better the "Characters" Wordsworth both perceives and writes, and which I take as implicating letters, people, and natural features. It will be hard to read them at such close range, but their terror and grandeur will be more visible. I quote from the last line of the above excerpt, Book VI, line 572, the third *s*, the one in *midst*. The *s* in *first* presents the birth of signification and would be too mythic; the *s* in *last* partakes of the finality of judgment after all the permutation of sense and sense-making has concluded—it would be too motionless. But the third *s*, fortuitously occurring in the middle of *midst*, displays in its curves the endlessly mediated social and material foundation upon which language meets the world. Perhaps some of the original rock, so ineffably suggestive, can be glimpsed behind the ink, beside it, or in its edges. The rock is moving; its motion through literary time shows up more clearly in print (Figure 3) than in handwriting. But don't take my word for it; turn the page and see—read—for yourself.

FOUR

Parataxis and Narrative: The New Sentence in Theory and Practice

"I'm new, said she, I don't think you'll find my card here . . . I'm new, said the oval moon. . . . I'm new, said the quartz crystal. . . . I'm new, said the mist rising from the duck pond. . . . I'm new, says the great dynamo."
—William Carlos Williams, *The Great American Novel*

Definitions

According to the old grammars, parataxis involves placing units together without connectives or subordination. "I came. I saw. I conquered." is paratactic;

> Of Man's First Disobedience, and the Fruit
> Of that Forbidden Tree, whose mortal taste
> Brought Death into the World, and all our woe,
> With loss of *Eden*, till one greater Man
> Restore us, and regain the blissful Seat,
> Sing Heav'nly Muse, that on the secret top
> Of *Oreb*, or of *Sinai*, didst inspire
> That Shepherd, who first taught the chosen Seed,
> In the Beginning how the Heav'ns and Earth
> Rose out of *Chaos*: Or if *Sion* Hill
> Delight thee more, and *Siloa's* Brook that flow'd
> Fast by the Oracle of God; I thence
> Invoke thy aid to my advent'rous Song,
> That with no middle flight intends to soar
> Above th' *Aonian* Mount, while it pursues
> Things unattempted yet in Prose or Rhyme.

is hypotactic. Hypotaxis involves grammatical subordination and one might think, making Milton paradigmatic, that grammatical subordination entails political and moral subordination as well. But thinking, which arrives, sees, conquers instantaneously, setting up empires in the blink of an eye, needs to be supplemented by reading, empirical, tortoise-like, always stuck in the provinces of a particular work, page, sentence. *Paradise Lost* may well counsel submission to authority, but its first sentence begins with disobedience and ends with Milton boasting.

In both Caesar's and Milton's world, rhetoric was a key human science, and parataxis one move among many in a verbal environment where expectations were highly codified. Parataxis of a more thorough and disorienting kind than anything the old handbooks could cite is the dominant if seemingly random mode of our time. It is hard to imagine escaping from atomized subject areas, projects, and errands into longer stretches of subjectively full narrative—not to mention a whole life. As targets of the media we are inundated by intense bursts of narrative-effect: a few seconds of heart-jerk in a life insurance ad (the wife looks longingly at the dead husband's smiling picture as she and the kids sadly leave the now-empty house), blockbuster miniseries four nights long, the six-month approach of the apotheosis of *Jurassic Park* or whatever major venture comes next. These sweeping affective beginnings and endings that shower upon us become visible as tightly managed packages when set against the corporate background that produces them. Those who teach literature (half of my presumed readers here, along with poets) might hope that they deal with more permanent, meaningful narratives, but such local totalities seem more than ever a relative affair—one's Joyce is another's Morrison is another's Hegel. Think of the standard Modern Language Association juxtapositions: "Androgyny in Chaucer" at 9:00 in the Wales Room; followed at 10:30 by "Yeats and Real Estate." Such titles make for easy jokes; the punchline is always the strained relation between literature and the world.

These obsessive spasms of narrative are symptoms of just how divided the present is. Spheres are separate (science, the arts); within spheres, fields are separate (poetry, music, sculpture); each field itself is balkanized; or, to switch from a geo-political to a financial metaphor, there are marketing niches. Even such choices in metaphor represent the parataxis that is ubiquitous in our sentences: spheres, fields, niches may be incommensurate shapes, but they are also densely interspersed. A map for poetry would contain language writing, Chicana poetry, academic poetry, cowboy poetry, workshop poetry, *et cetera*—there would always be an *et cetera* at the end of this or any other list. For many poets, the notion of personal autonomy—voice—makes an enclave from such atomization, as do the themes of love, loss, death, landscape, and seasonal time. Such themes present images of totality within their niche. The kind of literary parataxis I will be discussing can be totalizing, too, but since its broken surface is antinarrative it can seem to be a mere symptom of contemporary atomization. The tension between symptom and critique will be constant here.

The New Sentence

My focus will be "the new sentence," a term that is both descriptive of a writing procedure and, at times, a sign of literary-political proselytizing. While the theory behind the name is meant to politicize literature, the name itself smacks of common marketing practices: "the new Dodge," "the new Coke," "the New Frontier," "the New Covenant"—almost any noun can serve. Such overlaps do not necessarily signal any permanent discredit, however. The new sentence is both a symptom of the age and a formal device that is highly motivated by literary-historical concerns. It marks an attempt to move literature closer to daily life, which is certainly dominated by markets; at the same time, by equating the verse line and the prose sentence, it also marks the pursuit of a writing "unattempted yet in Prose or Rhyme."

The term was coined by Ron Silliman. While it was not a theoretical fiat—Silliman was analyzing writing that he and others had been producing—there was a sense in his discussion that the new sentence marked an advance in literary history.[1] Much more was at stake than a formal innovation: before introducing the new sentence, Silliman sketched the histories of linguistics, literary criticism, and poetry.[2] In fact, from a purely formal perspective, the new sentence was not that drastic an innovation. A new sentence is more or less ordinary itself, but gains its effect by being placed next to another sentence to which it has tangential relevance: new sentences are not subordinated to a larger narrative frame nor are they thrown together at random. Parataxis is crucial: the autonomous meaning of a sentence is heightened, questioned, and changed by the degree of separation or connection that the reader perceives with regard to the surrounding sentences. This is on the immediate formal level. From a larger perspective, the new sentence arises out of an attempt to redefine genres; the tension between parataxis and narrative is basic. Among other things, Silliman wanted to escape the problems of the novel, which for him were of a piece with the larger problems of capitalism:

> Freed from a recognition of the signifier and buffered from any response from an increasingly passive consumer, the supermarket novelist's language has become fully subservient to a process that would lie outside syntax: plot. The dynamic implicit in the novel's rise toward the illusion of realism is this divorce, conducted in stages over the centuries, of the tale

from the gravitational force of language. . . . This dream of an art with no medium, of a signified with no signifiers, is inscribed entirely within the commodity fetish.[3]

Accompanying this devaluation of the novel was an expansion of the definition of poetry. In "The Chinese Notebook," written at about the same time as the excerpt just quoted, Silliman insists that the series of Wittgensteinian prose meditations on poetry is itself poetry:

76. If I am correct that this is poetry, where is the family resemblance to, say, *The Prelude*? Crossing the Alps.

. . .

156. What if I told you I did not really believe this to be a poem? What if I told you I did?

. . .

179. How far will anything extend? Hire dancers dressed as security personnel to walk about an otherwise empty museum, then admit the public. Could this be poetry if I have proposed it as such?

. . .

220. When I return here to ideas previously stated, that's rhyme.[4]

"The Chinese Notebook" and the essays in *The New Sentence* were written in the seventies, when faith in the rebirth of modernist ambition and of the cultural centrality of poetry was easier to maintain than in the nineties. Today parataxis can seem symptomatic of late capitalism rather than oppositional. Ads where fast cuts from all "walks of life" demonstrate the ubiquity and omniscience of AT&T are paratactic. This similarity between the new sentence and current media practice has been pounced on rather gleefully by critics of language writing: "the stylistic gesture most characteristic of language writing is the non-sequitur. . . . It is the product of a generation raised in front of a television: an endless succession of depthless images and empty sounds, each cancelling the previous one. A non-sequitur implies a loss of memory, an erasing of history. 'Language' poetry as it is practiced by its strictest followers is identical to the speech of television's masterpiece, Ronald Reagan."[5] If Attention Deficit Disorder (ADD) had been a current term when this attack was made, doubtless it would have been included in the attacker's arsenal. New sentence writing can in fact require more attention rather than less from its readers, but if that attention is not granted, then the results might make a reader feel as if she was suffering from ADD. The bluntness of such an attack demonstrates that the new sentence claims a fundamentally different cultural function for poetry. Clearly, the nature of the units and the ways they are juxtaposed need to be considered before useful judgments can be made.

Judgments are being made, however, and not just in local poetry wars. As one of marks of the postmodern, parataxis has been yoked together with a host of cultural-literary terms in a basic controversy between parts and whole. On one side, there is narrative, totality, the subject, presence, depth, affect; and on the other, fragmentation, simulacra, schizophrenia, surface, pastiche, and, standing side by side with its allies (as it should, etymologically), parataxis. These literary, rhetorical, medical, philosophic and topographic terms are not, as readers of critical theory know, neutral. Fredric Jameson, in "The Cultural Logic of Late Capitalism," not only identifies language writing with the new sentence, but with depthlessness, Lacanian schizophrenia, the erasure of history, and the end of personal identity. Jameson's style, with its long periodic sentences, the clauses packed with qualification, seems far removed from such phenomena, but in the overall organization of its materials, his essay is itself paratactic: Andy Warhol's *Diamond Dust Shoes*, my poem "China," Michael Herr's *Dispatches*, the Bonaventura Hotel are among the units it yokes together. Jameson does not intend an easy moral denunciation of postmodernism—he almost celebrates it in places—but in discussing the parataxis in "China," his vocabulary registers significant alarm: he writes that when "the relationship [of signifiers to each other] breaks down, when the links of the signifying chain snap, then we have schizophrenia in the form of a rubble of distinct and unrelated signifiers."[6]

But we should examine this rubble more closely before language writing is swept wholesale into the depthless phalanx of postmodernism. While it may suggest fragmentation and schizophrenia to Jameson and others, in my experience, the new sentence had an import in the development of language writing that was precisely the opposite. Later, I will discuss "China" briefly; for now, I will cite the first few lines:

> We live on the third world from the sun. Number three. Nobody tells
>   us what to do.
>
> The people who taught us to count were being very kind.
>
> It's always time to leave.
>
> If it rains, you either have your umbrella or you don't.
>
> The wind blows your hat off.
>
> The sun rises also.[7]

What from one perspective may look like a sign of radical disconnection may from another be a gesture of continuity. For some, there may be utter gulfs between these sentences; others, however, may find narrative within any one of them and narrative linkages between them (the number three and counting; telling us what to do and teaching us; rain, wind, and sun). In the context out of which I was writing, each sentence of "China" seemed to me almost transgressively relaxed, prosy, novelistic.[8]

This was because, at the beginning of the language movement, the primary writing techniques or genres involved a high degree of syntactic and verbal fracturing. This writing was irregularly accompanied by much less fractured theories. Some such as Silliman with conscious Marxist critiques connected commodity and referential fetishism; others with less fluency in theory felt intuitional senses of the liberatory—or at least literary—potential of non-normative language. But given the cultural urgency felt by Marxists, lyricists, and syntactic guerrillas alike, the prevailing techniques and theories did not provide much possibility for direct statement.

For some language writers, working in complete sentences was one way to bring practice and daily life closer together. Writing in fragments might have kept one safely uncontaminated by the larger narratives of power, but to write in sentences was to use a publicly legible unit. Sentences per se were not the answer, however, as they were also being written by other poets who had quite different political and aesthetic aims. The following is an excerpt from a fairly widely circulated poetry anthology:

> Today I am envying the glorious Mexicans,
> who are not afraid to sit by the highway
> in the late afternoons, sipping tequila
> and napping beneath their wide sombreros
> beside the unambitious cactus. Today
> I am envying the sweet *chaparita* who waits
> for her lover's banjo in the drunken moonlight
> and practices her fingers against the soft tortilla.
> Today I am envying the green whiskers of God. . .[9]

The smug colonialism of this is offensive (like the old kitchen towels that say "Mañana"); but its main formal feature is not uncommon in much mainstream poetry: the poetry sentence, laden with adjectives ("glorious," "unambitious," "drunken"), verbal moods a sign of emotion (the repeated "I am envying"), nouns chosen for piquancy ("cactus," "*chaparita*," "banjo"). The incantatory lyricism of the poetry sentence, where writer finds voice and depoliticized universe fitting together without struggle, is an ideal environment for aggrandized sensitivity and myopic or minimized social context.

The new sentence, on the other hand, is defiantly unpoetic. Its shifts break up attempts at the natural reading of universal, authentic statements; instead they encourage attention to the act of writing and to the writer's multiple and mediated positions within larger social frames. The following is a small excerpt from Silliman's book-length poem, *Ketjak*:

> Those curtains which I like above the kitchen sink. Imagined lives we posit in the bungalows, passing, counting, with another part of the mind, the phone poles. Stood there broke and rapidly becoming hungry, staring at the nickels and pennies in the bottom of the fountain. Dear Quine, sentences are not synonymous when they mean the same proposition. How the heel rises and ankle bends to carry the body from one stair to the next. This page is slower. [10]

Making the sentence the basic unit of composition separates the writer from three widely held positions. First, it is arbitrary, driving a wedge between any expressive identity of form and content. What Silliman is doing goes directly against the grain of the poetics of "Projective Verse," where Olson gives primary place to Creeley's statement "FORM IS NEVER MORE THAN AN EXTENSION OF CONTENT."[11] In Silliman's case, form is clearly primary. But, secondly, to avoid a self-expressive stance does not then throw the writer into the arms of a trans-individual language. Foucault's statement may apply to some positions in language writing, but not to Silliman's: "The philosopher is aware . . . [that he] does not inhabit the whole of his language like a secret and perfectly fluent god. Next to himself, he discovers the existence of another language that also speaks and that he is unable to dominate, one that strives, fails, and falls silent and that he cannot manipulate."[12] Generating one sentence after another is, on the contrary, a sign of confident manipulation. A third distinction: to use the sentence as basic unit rather than the line is to orient the writing toward ordinary language use. Although collage is basic to the new sentence, the elements that are juxtaposed are quite different from those used in Ted Berrigan's *Sonnets*, where an emphatically artificial line not based on breath is the focal point:

> XV
>
> In Joe Brainard's collage its white arrow
> He is not in it, the hungry dead doctor.
> Of Marilyn Monroe, her white teeth white—

I am truly horribly upset because Marilyn
and ate King Kong popcorn," he wrote in his
of glass in Joe Brainard's collage
Doctor, but they say "I LOVE YOU"
and the sonnet is not dead.
takes the eyes away from the gray words,
Diary. The black heart beside the fifteen pieces
Monroe died, so I went to a matinee B-movie
washed by Joe's throbbing hands. "Today
What is in it is sixteen ripped pictures
does not point to William Carlos Williams.[13]

Number 15 is unique among Berrigan's 83 sonnets in that it can be 'un-collaged' by reading the lines in the following order: 1, 14; 2, 13; 3, 12, etc. Still, collage is the reigning principle here and not a mere baffle; it is crucial to the effect that lines end on hyphens and that capitals and quotation marks do not always make linear sense. But to display the materiality of language is not the goal: as is the case with much of Berrigan's writing, this is elegiac, and art is the ultimate consolation. Marilyn Monroe and William Carlos Williams have what eternal life they do because of Brainard's collage and Berrigan's art: "and the sonnet is not dead" is a cry of aesthetic resurrection. (Given Williams's disdain for sonnets, there's a touch of insurrection involved too.)[14]

Silliman makes no attempt to highlight the pathos (and humor) of a separation of art from life, or poetry from philosophy. Far from being fragments, his sentences derive from a coherent, wide-ranging political analysis. Contrary to Jameson's description of the new sentence, this writing seems to me self-critical, ambitiously contextualized, and narrative in a number of ways. In fact, Silliman's political analysis is quite similar to Jameson's; it is less nuanced, but to the extent that it factors in its own writing practice it is, in an essential dimension, wider. Many of the sentences are themselves brief narratives, but more important is the overall frame Silliman shares with Jameson: the Marxist master-narrative that sees commodification as a necessary stage that history must pass through. This master-narrative links what would otherwise be the very different levels of the sentences in the above excerpt: the domesticity of the kitchen with the spectacle of identical bungalows with the minute units of the pennies in the fountain with the small verbal differences between sentences that Quine ignores; the renter with the homeowner with the homeless person; housing policies with positivism with writing practices. Silliman's sense of the broken integers produced by capitalism is inseparable from his commitment to the emergence of a transformed, materialist society.[15]

The issue of literary quality is less important than the egalitarian politics of these sentences. Very ordinary ones are allowed in: "Those curtains which I like above the kitchen sink."[16]

New sentences imply continuity and discontinuity simultaneously, an effect that becomes clearer when they are read over longer stretches. In the following juxtaposition—"Fountains of the financial district spout soft water in a hard wind. She was a unit in a bum space, she was a damaged child" (3)—we have switched subjects between the sentences: the child and the fountains need not be imagined in a single tableau. This effect of calling forth a new context after each period goes directly against the structural impatience that creates narrative. It's as if a film were cut into separate frames. But in a larger sense, girl and fountain are in the same social space. Throughout the book, Silliman insists on such connections as the one between the girl and the wider economic realities implied by the corporate fountains. The damage that has been done to her has to be read in a larger economic context.

But we don't focus on the girl: she is one facet of a complex situation; she is not singled out for novelistic treatment. There's a dimension of tact involved: she's not representative of the wrongs done to children, but she's not given the brushoff either.[17] The degree of attention Silliman accords her can be read as analogous to the way one recognizes individuals in a crowd (as well as perceptions in a crowded urban setting), giving each a finite but focused moment of attention. This can be favorably compared to the generalized responses of Eliot and Wordsworth to London: phobia in the case of Eliot—"I had not thought death had undone so many"[18]—and despairing scorn in the case of Wordsworth, for whom urbanization resulted in minds "reduced to an almost savage torpor."[19] Of course, to compare Silliman to Eliot and Wordsworth can seem ill-proportioned to some; but if we can lay aside absolutist ideas of literary quality, then Silliman's writing can be read as an exemplary guide to contemporary urban life. The absence of an explicit plot serves it well in this capacity.

In fact, it is interesting to see Jameson, in another context, write that "new readers can be electrified by exposure to *Tarr*, a book in which, as in few others, the sentence is reinvented with all the force of origins, as sculptural gesture and fiat in the void. Such reinvention, however, demands new reading habits, for which we are less and less prepared."[20] While this sounds like praise for something close to the new sentence (as well as a call for the new reading habits the new sentence implies),[21] we should remember that the sum of Lewis's electrifying sentences is the novel *Tarr*, a narrative that Jameson reads as, among other things, a "national allegory," with Kreisler as Germany, Soltyk as Poland, Anastasya as Russia, all against the background of World

War I. In other words, he sees in Lewis's sentences a thoroughgoing homology between part and whole—even though in the same study he writes that "every serious practicing critic knows a secret which is less often publicly discussed, namely, that there exists no ready-made corridor between the sealed chamber of stylistic investigation and that equally unventilated space in which the object of study is reconstituted as narrative structure."[22] By refusing to construct larger narrative wholes beyond the provisional connections made at the time of the reading (or to put it another way, by making the reader re-narrativize), Silliman avoids the impasse Jameson mentions: with the new sentence there is no separation between style and plot, between reading at the level of the sentence and reading for narrative.

Silliman often attacks the homogeneity of large-scale narrative for drawing attention away from the materiality of the words on the page; the novel, to reiterate, is a primary target: "Details differ, / thus they mean"; "Narrative suppresses immediate attention"; "That each line is created equal / is contra-narrative."[23] Each new sentence is to reinvigorate verbal perception: where Jameson reads signifying chains snapping, Silliman reads the technicolor epics of false consciousness being swept away.[24] But alongside such de-narrativization, I want to emphasize (though Silliman often does not) that possibilities of re-narrativization are continually offered.

Even though his analysis omits it, one device that is crucial to his initial work with the new sentence is a highly developed structure of repetition. *Ketjak* is written in series of expanding paragraphs where the sentences of one paragraph are repeated in order in subsequent paragraphs with additional sentences inserted between them, recontextualizing them. As the paragraphs double, the space between the reoccurence of the sentences doubles and the context from which they reemerge grows thicker. In this, they have reminded some in the language movement of characters in a novel.[25] But the narrative effect is more peculiar as the sentences keep reappearing against different sentences. E.g.: "Look at that room filled with fleshy babies, incubating. We ate them." In the next paragraph: "Look at that room filled with fleshy babies. A tall glass of tawny port. We ate them." Next paragraph: "Look at that room filled with fleshy babies, incubating. Points of transfer. A tall glass of tawny port. The shadows between the houses leave the earth cool and damp. A slick gaggle of ambassadors. We ate them." The new sentence questions anaphora, so that reference is not guaranteed to extend beyond sentence boundaries. Thus "We ate," not babies, not port, not ambassadors, but only "them." On the other hand, Silliman is clearly enjoying the juxtapositions on his verbal or virtual smorgasbord. In moments like these, he seems to be playing a kind of *fort-da* game with readers' expectations for continuity.

In a more recent book, *What*, Silliman does not use repetition devices, thus embodying a more 'pure' degree of parataxis.[26] The results seem significantly different, though it will be hard to demonstrate this here, because a short excerpt will seem similar to the previous excerpts:

> The cash register makes a deeper tone
> if the Universal Product Code isn't picked up
> by the sensor. One after another,
> cars bounce in the pothole. . . .
>   "No on F,"
> "Stop dirty politics," giving no clue whatsoever
> what the issues might entail. (92–3)

These three sentences deal with the same content as before. Silliman is 'narrating' the story of the decontextualized units of late capitalism: grocery-store items, cars, bumper sticker slogans all passing through the grids of the service economy. But where in the earlier work the repetition and recombination of sentences distanced, framed, questioned, and at times ironized their contents; here, with no chance for recontextualization, the act of writing each sentence repeatedly pits writer against world (and against the mass of prior sentences), building up pressure for validity and for novelty, which can seem to merge with the story of cultural commodification against which the writing directs itself: the "new" of the new sentence is poised here between symptom and critique. In other words, can "One after another, / cars bounce in the pothole" be read as a description of the sentences themselves?

To suggest this is seemingly to circle back to Jameson's vision of the ahistorical anomie of postmodern schizophrenic production. But simply to homologize the cars and the sentences, the pothole and the experiential vacuum created by multinational capitalism would be to ignore the oppositional stance implicit in the sentences as they simultaneously depict and critique their world.

This critique is personal: a primary element of each sentence is the fact of Silliman writing. This surfaces in the many references to the physical act of writing; but it also appears in the content: for instance, one can follow, in separated but sequential sentences, the story of Silliman's marriage and his grandmother's death. At such times, the writing seems autobiographical, even though the narrative is focused more at the tip of the pen than in the memory of the writer. Larger narrative frames, theoretically repressed by Silliman's use of parataxis, clearly return, even within a single sentence. Consider the following:

I have flight (half-light). The audience
for poetry not being 'the masses' can be
quite specific—you choose the poem
or it chooses you (years later possibly
you meet the author at a party, a little, bald
bespectacled fellow, talking not art or politics
but baseball and gossip, the edges of everything
general and rounded) and your life is altered
irreparably by that decision, you change majors,
jobs, become passionate suddenly in ways
opaque to your lover, and frightening:
you didn't know poetry could be like that
but it's what you'd wanted all along,
so deeply in fact that you think for awhile
it might by genetic or that you were "destined"
as that poem seems also to have been destined
for a particular life, and maybe you are
and it was, if not in that sense in some other,
the way it has for all the others been just likewise,
each one choosing the poem, the poem choosing them,
even the ones who seem to you (for who are you
to judge?) completely muddied in what they do,
in how they think, the ones who publish
a single chapbook and get no response, no one
coming to their readings and they
going to fewer each year, writing less and
one day they realize they haven't even thought
of publishing in ages, the job is harder, the kids
demand time, and yet almost as if at random
copies of that chapbook dot the crowded shelves
of small used bookstores, just waiting
to be chosen and to choose, loaded
as a minefield. I heard mindfield. (94–95)

The length of the second sentence strikes me as exemplary of the unresolved pressure for narrative that Silliman's practice of the new sentence creates. This excerpt is not purely paratactic, as these three sentences are somewhat anaphoric. "Mindfield" refers back to "minefield"; and the various
anxieties over the success of careers, methods, and schools that stir so distur-
bingly through the elephantine sentence can be detected, in germ, in the tiny

pun of the first: have flight / half-light. Is one, as a poet, really flying with Pegasus or is one simply a dimwit? But these qualifications aside, the relatively complete commitment to parataxis in the later work also entails a commitment to Silliman's moral authority as a writer, since there is nothing else to motivate the appearance of the next new sentence. The long sentence is anomalous: nevertheless it demonstrates that the new sentence, by its freedom from older social narratives, creates euphoria ("your life is altered, you become passionate") while at the same time producing pressure to get everything—include life stories—said before the period.

The New Sentence and the Novel

I have been concerned here not to generalize: what I have written about Silliman does not apply as accurately to other language writers or, in fact, to some of his own books. I will turn now to the work of Lyn Hejinian. Her work is formally somewhat close to Silliman's, but it demonstrates that the new sentence can be used for quite different narrative and political-rhetorical effects, and that a new-sentence novel need not be such an unthinkable genre. The following passage is from *My Life*,

. . . . What were Caesar's battles but Caesar's prose. A name trimmed with colored ribbons. We "took" a trip as if that were part of the baggage we carried. In other words we "took our time." The experience of a great passion, a great love, would remove me, elevate me, enable me at last to be both special and ignorant of the other people around me, so that I would be free at last from the necessity of appealing to them, responding to them. That is, to be nearly useless but at rest. There were cut flowers in vases and ceramic bouquets, but in those days they did not keep any living houseplants. The old fragmentary texts, early Egyptian and Persian writings, say, or the works of Sappho, were intriguing and lovely, a mystery adhering to the lost lines. At the time, the perpetual Latin of love kept things hidden. It was not his fate to be as famous as Segovia. Nonetheless, I wrote my name in every one of his books. Language is the history that gave me shape and hypochondria. And followed it with a date, as if by my name I took the book and by the date, historically, contextualized its contents, affixed to them a reading. And memory a wall. My grandmother had been a great beauty and she always won at cards. As for we who "love to be astonished," the ear is less active than the eye. The artichoke has done its best, armored, with scales, barbed, and hiding in its interior the soft hairs so aptly called the choke. . . . Of course, one continues to write, and thus to "be a writer," because one has not yet written that "ultimate" work. Exercise will do it. I insert a description: of agonizing spring morning freshness, when through the open window a smell of cold dust and buds of broken early grass, of schoolbooks and rotting apples, trails the distant sound of an airplane and a flock of crows. I thought that for a woman health and comfort must come after love. Any photographer will tell you the same. So I wouldn't wear boots in the snow, nor socks in the cold. Shufflers scuff. That sense of responsibility was merely the context of the search for a lover, or, rather, for a love. Let someone from the other lane in. . . .[27]

Clearly, there is paratactic organization at work here, though recurrent attention to specific areas of memory makes the gaps between the sentences less didactic than is often the case with Silliman. The passage does, however, display a similar allegiance to the project of disrupting unities of poetic voice and narrative. A sentence containing only a bare metaphysical image ("And memory a wall"); a sentence of conventional reminiscence ("My grandmother . . . always won at cards"); a sentence mixing lyricism and aesthetics ("As for we . . . the ear is less active than the eye"): such a sequence foregrounds its artifice. The larger organization of the book does the same. In a gesture that is similar to many of Silliman's a priori procedural decisions, the first edition of *My Life*, written when Hejinian was thirty-seven, contains thirty-seven chapters of thirty-seven sentences each. The second edition, written eight years later, adds new chapters and inserts new sentences into earlier chapters to make forty-five chapters of forty-five sentences. So the sentence beginning "I insert a description," is a formal pun, since it is one of the new, second-edition sentences.

Nevertheless, the artificially inserted memory is emotional and lyrical. While not a traditional autobiography, *My Life* does not belie its title. Each chapter takes up—loosely, to be sure—a single year of Hejinian's life. I've quoted from the seventeenth chapter; once the frame of Hejinian at seventeen is placed around these sentences, quite a bit of the paratactic effect recedes, and a particular meditative and at times almost novelistic cast emerges. An adolescent hero-worship that admires Caesar, the father's library, "ultimate" masterpieces, is mixed with a budding awareness of sexuality. These strands unite closely in the intriguing lost lines of Sappho and the not-quite-decipherable "perpetual Latin of love." These complex senses can attach to most of the sentences. "Let someone from the other lane in," can be read as referring to a moment of traffic contemporaneous with the writer's present and thus as a paratactic jump; but it also can be read as a metaphor for the expansion of literary-erotic sympathies that the passage as a whole continually glances at. Sometimes an artichoke is just an artichoke, but it can also be an image of emergent sexuality quite appropriate to adolescence, both unopened bud, and armored Joan of Arc.

The intermittent past tense helps establish this quasi-narrative coherence: again, once the frame is suggested, a little can go a long way. But throughout the book Hejinian also keeps the present moment of the writing in the foreground. At times she keeps her younger self at a critical distance, as when the older writer comments caustically on the seventeen-year-old's desire for a great passion: "That is, to be nearly useless but at rest." But writing and prior experience are more often mixed. From the twentieth chapter:

> What memory is not a "gripping" thought. Only fragments are accurate. Break it up into single words, change them to combination. So we go into the store shopping and get, after awhile, you know, contralto! Thinking about time in the book, it is really the time of your life. I was experiencing love, immensely relieved. It was, I know, an unparticular spirit of romance. She apologizes and seizes us in the grip of her inadequacies. Giving the back-up o.k. to the loaded semi. (55)

The first sentence is most easily read as present-time meditation; the shopping sentence, on the other hand, seems pure reenactment (and is about as close as Hejinian ever gets to Valley talk). In "It was, I know, an unparticular spirit of romance" both times exist: "I know" and most likely the allusion to Pound's *Spirit of Romance* belong to the time of writing; but the feeling of being caught up by standard-issue feelings belongs to Hejinian's twentieth year. The next sentence switches to the third person and critiques the prior sentence: "[Since she now finds her early romance boring,] She apologizes and seizes us in the grip of her inadequacies." The goal is for writing and living to be continuous: "Thinking about time in the book, it is really the time of your life." A more comic presentation of the multiple acts of this writing— remembering, reliving, and creating—occurs in the image of the loaded semi and the person standing behind supervising its backing-up.

In a later book, *Oxota: A Short Russian Novel*,[28] the relationship between the sentences and their narrative burden is complex in different ways. As the title suggests, Hejinian does not seem fazed to approach the problematic genre, the novel. But the book is far from a conventional novel; it is hardly a record of Hejinian's time in what was then Leningrad: only the vaguest chronicle can be constructed from the almost 300 fourteen-line poems (referred to as "sonnets" on the back cover in a gesture toward the sonnets that make up Pushkin's *Evgeny Onegin*). But the opacity of external event does not lead back to the sense that language is a privileged entity. In this *Oxota* is quite different from Silliman's writing. The root of Silliman's political aesthetics is faith in language as the site of an active community, not inheriting meanings but creating them through precise acts of reading and writing, most aptly exemplified in the lines quoted in Chapter Two: "The point at which you read each word (the / only point there is), two minds share a larger whole."[29] But *Oxota* does not display any larger wholes: the line is a provisional unit, always ending without a period. The construction of rudimentary interpretation and identity are predominant. Two minds share a two-sided conundrum:

Chapter Eighty-Nine

Misha should be a major character in the Russian novel
Sasha, too, and Nadia
You will start with the third chapter, Arkadii said, and the first
    sentence must be attributed to Emmanuel Kant as follows:
    everything happens so often, that speaking of it makes no sense
You will meet people accompanying their ghosts, said Alyosha, and
    speak with them
Kolya, Shura, Borik, Sveta, Tanya, Natasha, Igor, Vladik, Vanya,
    and the other Misha
Zina stood on a chair
Arkadii waved the ghosts aside
There must be a sentence which claims a chapter for itself
And a name at the vanishing point in a person's description
So that the days will seem not to have gone by—and in fact names
    are relationships with a remarkable economy while descriptions
    are profligate
But pleasure is a mental process too as well as the producer of an
    aesthetic object
It is not what I knew
Our Russian workers like to dig holes, Arkadii said, while
    Americans prefer machines that scoop
The coincidence of experiences occurring with experiences already
    had produced identity—but it spills (101)

Arkadii, or whoever pronounces the eighth line, seems to ask that "the Russian novel" (i.e., *Oxota* itself, whose production is discussed in many of the poems[30]) contain something like the new sentence: "a sentence which claims a chapter for itself." But while *Oxota* is more or less paratactic from line to line, the lines themselves gesture toward a continuity with their Russian surroundings in a spirit that is much different from the new sentence.

Leningrad, a collaborative account of a prior trip to the Soviet Union written by Hejinian, Silliman, Barrett Watten, and Michael Davidson, records a Russian saying to Silliman: "You speak as one who comes from a land of objects, therefore it is easy for you to conceive of language as an object, as objective, whereas we do not."[31] The generalization that writers of the West do not see language as subjective seems odd in the light of the widespread commitment in poetry to authenticities of the self; nevertheless, this remark is suggestive in that the new sentence can be seen as arising out specifically of a culture of consumerism.[32] This does not automatically mean, however, that the parataxis of language writing is automatically equivalent to shopping or channel surfing: to repeat, parataxis can be used oppositionally. But *Oxota* demonstrates one way parataxis operates in a context of scarcity. In the West, overloads of objects, viewpoints, schools, channels, typefaces, marketing strategies create pressure which can make the sequential coherence and drama of the novel seem like Victorian coincidence. In the world of *Oxota*, on the other hand, there is not enough of anything: chickens, paper, living space are constantly being sought; connection itself becomes a luxury and metaphorical extravangazas fill the gaps between things: "Ostap pointed toward a slab of frying spam and said, that organism is what we call fruit" (47).

Rather than an exact instrument to create a utopian textual politics as with Silliman, in *Oxota* language continually verges on the comic. Each word is foreign, deliberately nonauthoritative:

> Upstairs I met with Evgenii Ivanovich, who was translating the
>   American metaphorist Raymond Chandler
> A pale man with a tiny pad
> He turned away and lifted its page
> What does it mean, please, "The woman has rubber lips with no
>   tread"
> She's lost her grip on the truth
> Or maybe what she says goes by him
> We have no such metaphors, he said, but maybe I'll find one
> Maybe something like, "The circle she made with her mouth was
>   warped" (198)
> . . . .
>
> In the Hermitage there was no coffee
> Cunt of weakness! an American mumbled carefully, reading
>   transliteration from a handy traveller's book
> There was an original resemblance and the young painter slashed it
> No coffee, no cold, no hole in this reality, Liuda said

> We had descended—tea must be without feminism
> It was a terrible thing—a great separation—this young painter's knife
>   had a butterfly's wings
> But it is our feminism to recall the village, Liuda said (193)

Comedy is not the main point, however. The mixed diction of "What does it mean, please, 'The woman has rubber lips with no tread'" could make for a punchline; but the passage goes beyond it to a provisionally effective translation. Neither the classic (or 'classic'—it hardly matters) American language of Chandler nor the foreignness of the Russian's English is allowed a settled status. Rather, as the end of Chapter 53 puts it: "The excitation of the same experience by two grammars—it's not impossible" (63). Silliman's credo makes any one point of language absolute: "the only point there is"; here the words are a provisional place of initial contact of different cultures and languages. *Oxota* seems poised between the West's late capitalism and the peculiar status of Russia in 1990, where there is no settled social system: hence rhetoric and genre are not fixed either.

Franco Moretti, among others, has shown how the novel was an element in the construction of the nation state in the eighteenth and nineteenth centuries.[33] If one accepts this, then one can find in the rapid exactitude of the new sentence a way of drawing useful maps in a postnational (and postnovel) environment—at least, to the extent that the new sentence is motivated by an ethic of activist prodding. *Oxota* demonstrates a way of reacting to a more uncertain situation. Some of characters in the book evoke prenovelistic images of village folktale motifs with great longing—"grannies"; "great Siberian soup," etc.—but these are not certainties that Heijinan hopes to recapture. "But it is our feminism to recall the village"—which way does that read? It is poised between a cosmopolitan Western feminism and a rural patriarchy, articulating an unstable territory where American English has no claim to authority; it is simply an interested onlooker.

De-narrativization and Re-narrativization

To care for the readings I have tried to sketch here requires a commitment to unities that are provisionally autonomous: poetry, language writing, the work of individual language writers. Such qualifications need to be set back into a more totalized context, however. It is of value, in other words, to set the new sentence beside postmodern architecture and television, as Jameson does. But any specific work using the new sentence will lose focus if it is not read with some attention to the original context, even though in the case of language writing that context (poetry) is itself called into question.

Discontinuity or continuity in writing results from complex conditions of reading. Whitman's paratactic catalogs seemed bizarre and discontinuous to most of his contemporaries, yet for this century's readers they are more likely to suggest connection and a totalizing embrace of society. (One can see a doppleganger of this embrace in the economically calculated shots in the ads I alluded to at the beginning: the airline pilot, the old couple, the stockbroker, the black construction worker, the waitress, and so on. There is often a patriotic subplot in these ads that also recalls Whitman.)[34] Novels, on the other hand, which would seemingly be connected narrative by definition, can register as paratactic in a number of ways. Camus's use of the *passé composé* in *The Stranger* is commonly pointed out to students of French as a mark of discontinuity: "What," asks *Cliff's Notes*, "does [Mersault's] habit of not relating events to one another tell us about his character?"[35] And the sentence-by-sentence writing in *Bouvard and Pecuchet*—as well as the plot as a whole—is comic precisely because there is no contact between items that are supposedly in immediate connection with one another. Bouvard & Pecuchet's pedantic steps toward understanding the world lead nowhere.

> First what is beauty?—For Schelling, it is the infinite expressing itself in the finite; for Reid, an occult quality; for Jouffroy, a fact incapable of analysis; . . . .
>
> And there exist several kinds of beauty: a beauty of science, geometry is beautiful; a beauty of behavior, it cannot be denied that the death of Socrates was beautiful. A beauty of the animal kingdom: the beauty of the dog consists in its sense of smell. A pig could not be beautiful on account of its filthy habits; nor a snake, because it awakes in us ideas of baseness.
>
> Flowers, butterflies, birds may be beautiful. In fact the first condition of beauty is unity in variety; that is the root of the matter.
>
> 'Yet,' said Bouvard, 'two cross-eyes are more varied than two ordinary ones and produce a less good effect, as a rule.'
>
> They entered upon the question of the sublime.[36]

Each sentence or phrase here is something of a "new sentence," though for a very different purpose than is the case with Silliman or Hejinian. The elementary completeness of each little pronouncement here is the result of authoritarian abbreviation. The ironic gaps that Flaubert wants us to read between each assertion reveal the lunatic abyss underlying the pedagogical narrative of organized knowledge. The lack of necessary connection is a cause for ultimate despair on Flaubert's part; for Hejinian and Silliman it creates an opening for the next new sentence.

I should remark here that the rhetorical tone of "China"—to my mind one of the salient features of the poem—is the opposite of the irony in *Bouvard and Pecuchet*: the poem touches on the matter-of-fact utopian feelings that early education can evoke.[37] The opening line—"We live on the third world from the sun. Number three. Nobody tells us what to do."—combines rudimentary astronomy with an assertion of complete independence, as if learning about the solar system in second grade marks a liberation from older narratives of fate. But despite the ingenuous tone of the poem, irony does appear in the assertions of collectivity. Nobody (from other planets or from heaven) tells us what to do: but that doesn't mean that "we" don't tell each other what to do. The same tension appears in a subsequent line such as "Everyone enjoyed the explosions." It means one thing if "everyone" refers to a rural village celebrating the new year with firecrackers; there is solidarity, camraderie. But if the context is the Vietnam War, the meaning changes: the explosions now are deadly, and "everyone" loses its communal character, and embodies colonialist violence. Recall one of the etymological roots of parataxis: soldiers standing side by side. Paratactic composition can bring up this major conundrum of contemporary society: are we on the same side, or are we each in separate armies in the war of "all against all"?

Let me conclude by reiterating that Jameson and Silliman both make wide theoretical claims; both are trying to fight the random parataxis of commodification with a more committed, oppositional parataxis—the positing of structural similarities across categories. While Hejinian's use of parataxis coexists more amiably with narrative, her sentences are also committed to breaking up any smooth narrative plane. De-narrativization is a necessary part of construction in these wider paratactic arguments. But this process needs to be seen for the combined reading and writing practice that it is: re-narrativization is also necessary. If we try to separate out the results of these practices, we are left with fictions, metaphorical condensations: the purely autonomous, politically efficacious new sentence on the one hand, and the rubble of snapped signifying chains on the other.

FIVE

Write the Power: Orthography and Community

Poetry and the Academy

It's an old joke. In John Cage's retelling, it goes like this:

Ramakrishna said:

Given a choice between going to heaven
and hearing a lecture on heaven, people
would choose the lecture.[1]

This bitter gibe at the failure of the transcendent to make a direct mark on society can be applied to many contexts; I want to let Cage's use of lines suggest poetry in place of heaven: not a surprising substitution, as poets have claimed a direct access to the divine for millennia. The joke would then illustrate a common gripe poets have about the hegemony of criticism and the marginalization of poetry within the academy. But not all poets accept their heavenly, marginal position. This is especially true of the work of Charles Bernstein; and I will turn briefly to the work of the Caribbean poet Edward Kamau Brathwaite as a interestingly oblique comparison. In both cases, poetry and theory, nonsense and explanation, febrillity and power will turn out to be deeply intermixed. As a token of this intermingling, I want to point out that, though Cage's lines seem to valorize heaven, the frame "Ramakrishna said" makes the lines themselves into a mini-lecture.

Issues of genre and institutional hierarchy are essential to the work of Bernstein, who has become the language writer best known to the academy.[2] Along with Andrews, McCaffery, Silliman, and Watten, he has been one of the leading theorists of the group. One could say that the publication of his latest book of essays, *A Poetics*, by a major university press marks a significant acknowledgment of language writing by institutionalized literary criticism. One could say that the center has opened an embassy in an exotic territory. But in *A Poetics* Bernstein does not write simply as an ambassador for the formerly marginalized language movement, but aims for more utopian conjunctions made possible through writing: he envisions a loosely confederated republic whose politics would be informed by a noncentralized, non-hierarchical poetry (although, to reiterate, Bernstein's sense of "poetry" is opposed to its usage in creative-writing contexts, where implications of craft and sensibility reign). The founding mothers and fathers of this republic would include Swinburne, Wilde, Dunbar, Hughes, Riding, Stein, and Zukofsky; experimental women's and African-American writing are among its potential constituencies, as are a number of tendencies in theory. In places, Bernstein claims poetry as the prime theoretical instrument; one long essay is written in verse, and throughout the book, metaphorical overloads and gusts of punning, malaprop humor arise unpredictably in the midst of theoretical discussion. But this potential republic faces major structural problems: the multicultural literary politics suggested at times are not well supported by the extremes of poetic singularity continually insisted on; this singularity also throws the promised merger of poetry and poetics into question.

Bernstein's continual humor—certainly a pleasure in the critical landscape—and the finesse with which he traverses institutional contexts (contemporary photography and painting, TV news and ads, video games, poststructuralism) mask the intransigence that ultimately informs the book where poetry is concerned. A small typographical feature can serve as an initial symptom. On the front and back covers, the half-title and title pages, and in the paragraph giving the Library of Congress publication data, the book's title is *A Poetics*. But on one page before the text begins, *a p o e t i c s* is printed in evenly spaced lowercase bold letters. This doppleganger embodies a key property of the book: *a p o e t i c s* with its nonhierarchical typography (no capital letters, no word boundaries) is a small sample of the radically democratic poetry Bernstein is arguing for, a poetry not governable by a normative poetics, a poetry that would itself constitute an apoetics. The evenly spaced letters recall the title of the journal edited by Bernstein and Bruce Andrews in the seventies and eighties, $L=A=N=G=U=A=G=E$, where, like the negative semiosis of *a p o e t i c s*, the construction made by the letters both points at and excludes itself from its constitutive category. In language, there is no word $L=A=N=G=U=A=G=E$. To bring out this aspect of Bernstein's apoetics more clearly I will look beyond *A Poetics* to a poem of his, "A Defence of Poetry," where the marriage of poetry and poetics is enacted much more thoroughly than in the book and, at the same time, the divorce is all the more explosive. While the book champions marginal poetry and does so in ways that tweak senses of mainstream critical decorum, it is still legible and, one could almost say, conciliatory to the mainstream. The poem, "A Defence," is much more defiantly illegible. The distance to which this second critique goes in order to remain inassimilable is remarkable and will, I think, shed quite a bit of light on the institutional situation of poetry. Consonant with the self-marginalization of the poem is the fact that it appears in a venue which, from a mainstream perspective, is inconspicuous: *Aerial*, a small-press magazine published irregularly out of Washington,D.C.—but, as we shall see, far from the site of government. First, however, a look at the poetry-poetics-politics announced in, if not fully enacted by, *A Poetics*.

Poetry as a Counter-State

Bernstein frames the book with gestures that make poetry a counter-State or non-State. The opening declares, "There is of course no state of American poetry" (1); the final exhortation is "Hold your own hearings" (228). These statements outline the political territory Bernstein claims: there is no state and it governs by singular, nonnormative judgments. If one had to pick out a slogan to appear on the currency, perhaps the following would do: "The violence of every generalization crushes the hopes for a democracy of thoughts" (113).

Metaphoric politics occur throughout, but the specific effect of poetry in contemporary society is a more consistent polemical concern. Normative language is the target: Bernstein opposes all "structures, styles, tropes, methods of transition" (225) that enforce standardization. But dismissing normative writing leaves no other role for poetry than the negative one of reacting against the center. When it comes to positing a public function for poetry, Bernstein is much more tentative, admitting "it's almost a joke to speak of poetry and national affairs. Yet . . . Rousseau writes that since our conventions are provisional, the public may choose to reconvene in order to withdraw authority from those conventions that no longer serve our purposes. Poetry is one of the few areas where the right of reconvening is exercised" (225).

Such public suggestions have a short half-life, as Bernstein tends to ironize them or to retreat into marginal, small-press areas of suggested action. There is little stable sense of a public that might decide to write and rewrite its own poems: how could there be when there is no settled sense of poetic discourse? Dissidence breaks into parodies of centralizing forms or separates itself from power; "Poets don't have to be read, any more than trees have to be sat under, to transform poisonous societal emissions. . . . As a poet, you affect the public sphere with each reader, with the fact of the poem, and by exercising your prerogative to choose what collective forms you will legitimate. The political power of poetry is not measured in numbers; it instructs us to count differently" (226).

The contradiction in the first sentences can be softened if we understand "Poets don't have to be read" to imply "Poets don't have to be widely read," which is a point Bernstein makes consistently as he argues against the ideas of "a common standard of aesthetic judgment" and "the value of a common readership" (5), favoring instead the singular act of writing. But in considering reading and the public sphere, some sense of number has to obtrude. Bernstein's pervasive antagonism to all forms of generalization undermines the "legitimation of collective forms," which makes "the political power of poetry" operate only on the particular, not to say, the atomized reader. Bernstein's political counting system uses two numbers: a centralized One and a plural non-one, with any specific number above one constituting a moral dilemma. The opening essay, "State of the Art," defines poetry as irreducibly plural: *"Poetry is the aversion of conformity"* (1).

The model oscillates between a writing that unites opposites and a writing that refuses identity. Occasionally Bernstein envisions a capacious unity, as in his call for "a poetry and a poetics that do not edit out so much as edit in. . . . A poetry—a poetic—that expresses the states of the art as it moves . . . beyond the modern and the postmodern" (2). But such unities of poetry and poetics, modern and postmodern—*e pluribus unum*—flip into their opposite. Instead of an enlarged identity serving as an umbrella organization for various specific constituencies united in nonhierarchical fashion, writing becomes the site of an intimate demonstration of the impossibility of identity.

> I think of Edmond Jabès's comment that a Jew, in his remarkable sense that Jewishness is the condition of writing, is always in exile, even in her own words.
>
> I want to raise the implicit error in these lines of reasoning because one of the main things I want to suggest is that poetics must necessarily involve error. Error in the sense of wandering, errantry, but also error in the sense of mistake, misperception, incorrectness, contradiction. Error as projection (expression of desire unmediated by rationalized explanation): as slips, slides . . . .
>
> I am interested . . . to put into talks like this, essays, certain kinds of pratfalls . . . slipping on a banana, or throwing a pie in my own face. (153–54)

A poetry-poetics-politics of the self-estranging self coexists uneasily with any multicultural affirmation. Bernstein affirms difference—Northumbrian dialect in Bunting's poetry; African-American vernacular in Dunbar; sexualized artifice in Wilde; utopianism in Morris—but he opposes representativeness, since the literary establishment translates the representative into an assimilative tokenism, as the following parodies show:

The works selected to represent cultural diversity are those that accept the model of representation assumed by the dominant culture in the first place. "I see grandpa on the hill / next to the memories I can never recapture" is the base line against which other versions play: "I see my yiddishe mama on Hester street / next to the pushcarts I can no longer peddle" or "I see my grandmother on the hill / next to all the mothers whose lives can never be recaptured" or "I can't touch my Iron Father / who never canoed with me / on the prairies of my masculine epiphany." (6)

The first and the third of the parody variations show Bernstein's shrewdly polemical humor. The pushcarts on Hester Street refer to the Pushcart Press, which publishes collections of formally conventional small-press writing, thus (mis)representing marginality in mainstream fashion. The Iron Father indicates Robert Bly's Iron John, the New Age male icon of privileged self-help. But the grandmother parody isn't particularly funny, indicating the difficulty in the political function Bernstein assigns poetry.

Confronted with the flat sententiousness of *Iron John*'s prairies where no irony is visible for miles, Bernstein reacts with a semantic monkey wrench typical of his poetry: "canoeing across the prairie." But the grandmother parody targets a personal narrative, "my grandmother," different from those entailed by such commodifications as "grandpa" or "memories." "All the mothers" is a political generalization that in some contexts could well be derived from specific lives. Bernstein's irony attacks commodified representations of groups, but not group poetics.

Turning from the politics of *A Poetics* to its poetics or apoetics, we will find a similar dynamic: clarity in attack and diffuse positive statements. Bernstein criticizes the centralized target of what he has called "official verse culture"[3]—the nexus of poets and critics who enforce norms of poetic value based on transparent language, but what he offers instead is defined by ambiguity. He attacks Helen Vendler's habit, in her introduction to *The Harvard Book of Contemporary Verse*, of "referring to what 'all' poems do":

> Vendler says
> she hopes readers will be provoked by some of the anthologized
>   poems to say—
> " 'Heavens, I recognize
> the place, I know it!' It is the effect every poet
> hopes for."

The poem Vendler singles out is Elizabeth Bishop's "Poem," a meditation on what Bishop discovers to be a painting by her grandfather. It is a well-crafted example in poetic animation: like the contemporaneous "Instruction Manual" of John Ashbery, it starts from a lifeless representation which it then enters and animates. A basic difference is that Ashbery's poem ends with a de-animation of the scene,[4] while Bishop, though keeping us conscious of the materials of the painting she is contemplating, leaves us in its vividness. (A further distinction is also important: Bishop's "Poem" depends on a personal inheritance, whereas the fantasy of "The Instruction Manual" is rooted in bureaucratic materials.) To anticipate my argument, this choice exemplifies two terms of Bernstein's I will discuss in a moment, "artifice" and "absorption." These are not starkly binary oppositions. The Bishop poem foregrounds the artificiality of the painting's representation in a number of lines, such as: "a wild iris, white and yellow, / fresh-squiggled from the tube." The moment of recognition Vendler celebrates is surrounded by similar touches:

> A specklike bird is flying to the left.
> Or is it a flyspeck looking like a bird?
>
> Heavens, I recognize the place, I know it!
> It's behind—I can almost remember the farmer's name.
> His barn backed on that meadow. There it is,
> titanium white, one dab.[5]

But recognition of the shabby constructions of art gives all the more strength to Bishop's celebration of the moments of transport that art can provide. She sees "Life and the memory of it cramped, / dim, on a piece of Bristol board, / dim, but how live." This mixed blessing is "the little that we get for free, / the little of our earthly trust." The moment of recognition is where the poem wants to abide, as it ends: "the iris, crisp and shivering, the water / still standing from spring freshets, / the yet-to-be-dismantled elms, the geese." Not to denigrate Bishop's poem, but it does seem problematic that a moment steeped in nostalgia (however nobly kept at bay) would serve Vendler as the exemplar for "Contemporary American Poetry" and that the line she singles out would be precisely the one likely to date soonest: "Heavens" (especially when accompanied by an exclamation mark) is not that far in tone from "Egad!" A final comment before picking up Bernstein's argument again: it is interesting that Bishop's "Poem" is about an amateur production. It begins, "About the size of an old-style dollar bill, / . . . this little painting has never made any money in its life." Compare the aesthetic, not just social, involvement of Ashbery and O'Hara with the decidedly professional New York art scene.

Bernstein's commentary continues:

> I would hope
> readers might be provoked to say of *some* poems,

"Hell, I don't recognize the place or the time or
the 'I' in this sentence. I don't know it." (42)

The irony directed against Vendler's values is unmistakable, but what is affirmed receives a larger dose of irony. Bernstein's writing has to avoid self-
definition or be convicted of the violence of generalization.

To avoid this violence, stability of genre is sacrificed. The excerpt could be
poetry, prose, or neither. It looks like poetry but the rhetoric and subject are
expository, and the line breaks are insignificant. Such blurring is the point: "if
there's a temptation to read the long essay-in-verse . . . as prose, I hope there
will be an equally strong temptation to read the succeeding prose as if it were
poetry" (3).

But "poetry" must remain undefined. If it is the task of poetics to furnish
portable, stable analytic terms, then *A Poetics* is committed to an apoetics.
Bernstein does, however, gesture toward terminology. The essay in verse,
"Artifice of Absorption," invokes Bataille's restrictive and general economies, and makes extensive use of Michael Fried's term, absorption, contrast-
ing it with impermeability. These two sets of oppositions differentiate persua-
sive writing from writing that foregrounds its own formality; Bernstein's
allegiance is to the side of the binary less valued by conventional poetics. But
it is not a rigorous commitment. The very idea of an invariable term smacks of
the exactitude of a restrictive economy. Potential sites of definition become
loci for counter-demonstrations of a writing practice that disrupts any form of
containment:

> By *absorption* I mean engrossing, engulfing
> completely, engaging, arresting attention, reverie
> attention intensification, rhapsodic, spellbinding,
> mesmerizing, hypnotic, total, riveting,
> enthralling: belief, conviction, silence.
>
> *Impermeability* suggests artifice, boredom,
> exaggeration, attention scattering, distraction,
> digression, interruptive, transgressive,
> undecorous, anticonventional, unintegrated, fractured,
> fragmented, fanciful, ornately stylized, rococo,
> baroque, structural, mannered, fanciful, ironic,
> iconic, schtick, camp, diffuse, decorative,
> repellent, inchoate, programmatic, didactic,
> theatrical, background muzak, amusing: skepticism,
> doubt, noise, resistance. (29–30)

These definitions, especially the second, work against any sense of definitiveness: "programmatic" and "inchoate" are a difficult yoking; as are "camp" and "didactic"; and "background muzak" and "transgressive." (Though to write trivia deliberately could be transgressive—but is the repeat of "fanciful" to be read as "transgressive"? "diffuse"? "mannered"? "repellent"?)

Such queries are the worries of an accountant for a restricted economy of meaning. A nonaccountant for a general economy can be more creative when doing his books. Here is another of Bernstein's definitions of absorption: "So we can speak of a bloated poem, / or a burst text, adding evaluative qualification: / well bloated or bloated but blundering; exquisitely / burst or dismally popped; elegantly engorged or / haplessly logorrheic" (23). "Blundering," "dismally," "haplessly" do not imply "bad"; the negative connotations exist as refugees from the evaluative wordscape of a restricted economy; the earnestness is comic in a general economy where an "equal" amount of pleasure— but who's counting?—is present in contemplating the idea of a poem "elegantly engorged" as in one "haplessly logorrheic." The rhythm of "exquisitely / burst" makes a close parallel to "dismally popped," thus equating— general economy style—the two adverbs. The rhythmic play and alliteration add to a nice send-up of "poetry"—or of blurb-prose or wine-talk.

Bernstein floats free of restrictive terminology in faux-generalizing passages such as these, but he does evaluate when it comes to specific poems, styles, and careers: e.g., his attack on Vendler; or in these lines on Allen Ginsberg and Louis Simpson, where the assumptions are different than in the impermeable-list: "Causal unity is often motivated by a desire / to create more absorbing, 'effective' / poems. The problem is that often / it doesn't work; the devices employed / create poems that seem phony / or boring or / uncompelling. . . . / . . . simplistic / notions of absorption through unity, [are] / . . . sometimes put forward by Ginsberg / (who as his work shows / knows better, but who has made an ideological / commitment to such simplicity) & Simpson / (whose case is less complex)" (38–39).

Here "phony / or boring or / uncompelling" does mean "bad." This is specific literary politics: unlike Simpson, who is dismissed, Ginsberg receives nuanced treatment, as Bernstein critiques him while keeping diplomatic channels open. Even though its line breaks foreground its artifice, the poem-essay contains much conventional writing. A large part of it is devoted to an omnibus review of contemporary poetry, providing capsule summaries of a number of language writers: "In Peter Seaton's poems the eclipsing / of a hard-to-absorb syntax with the absolute / current & dynamism of compositional flow / reaches majestic proportions" (61).

"Artifice" provides information on writing not yet well known to the academy, performing what I consider a useful service. (This is not a neutral remark: my work is among that considered.) My point is, however, that such tactical maneuvering in the context of publication and evaluation cannot be derived from, and in fact goes directly against, Bernstein's conception of nonhierarchical poetry. But the contradiction is constitutive; an unpositionable poetry makes an effective institutional base. "[P]oetry is the trump; [it] has the power to absorb these other forms of writing, but these other forms do not have that power over poetry . . . [P]oetry . . . can't be contained by any set of formal qualities, while, in contrast, one might be able to read novels or letters or scientific treatises in terms of *their* poetic qualities. . . . Or else I imagine poetics as an invasion of the poetic into other realms" (150–51).

Here poetry cannot be pinned down but can operate in other institutionally defined spaces. Bernstein opposes absorption in poetry—the transparent workshop poem—but antiabsorptive poetry can absorb, in an institutional sense, all other forms of writing.

Liberated Textuality

Here is the opening of "A Defence of Poetry," which displays the stresses of Bernstein's poetic utopianism compactly.

A Defence of Poetry

My problem with deploying a term liek
nonelen
in these cases is acutually similar to
your
cirtique of the term ideopigical
unalmlsing as a too-broad unanuajce
interprestive proacdeure.
You say too musch lie a steamroller when
we need dental (I;d say jeweller's)
tools.
(I think youy misinterpret the natuer of
themaic
interpretatiomn of evey
evey detail in every peim
but an oeitnetation towatd a kind of
texutal practice
that you prefer to call "nksense" but
for *poltical* purpses I prepfer to call
ideological!
(say, Hupty Dempty)

This enunciates a basic tension between reading and writing. To write it is one thing, but to read it involves translation, conscious or subliminal: "My problem with deploying a term like nonsense." But the translated poem will warn, in subsequent lines, against translating. The conflict between legibility and creativity is also rehearsed in the difference between the title, a well-formed phrase with an impeccable literary pedigree, and the poem. In fact, to call this a poem glosses over its challenge to conventional definitions of poetry. It is signifying, in Henry Louis Gates's sense, on such definitions. The dynamics of self-estrangement in language that *A Poetics* displayed are here extended to the structure of single words, so the central nonterm, "nonsense," appears first as "nonelen" and "nksense."

Bernstein recommends an omnivorous, nonjudgmental process that would read without evaluating. But the surface of the poem flirts with the judgmental category of error. Doesn't *"poltical,"* especially italicized, act out a kind of slapstick? Can "the *poltical* is the political" be taken as an unironic lesson? By defacing language so assiduously, Bernstein here separates himself from most twentieth-century poets, including language writers such as Silliman, Hejinian, and Watten, whose work demonstrates variegated commitments to precision, cultural specificity, and even lyricism.

A possible line of descent for "A Defence" would include Dada, the writings of Abraham Lincoln Gillespie and Elsa von Freytag-Loringhoven, and *Finnegans Wake*. But the poem is more argumentative than Dada; less committed to an iconoclastic social role for the poet than Freytag-Loringhoven; and its orthography has not been twisted to suggest some dreamscape of multiple signification as in Gillespie's work or in *Finnegans Wake*: these are typos, dull demons of one's own bodily clumsiness. *eik* instead of *ike* makes "leik"; semicolon instead of apostrophe makes "I;d." We are all familiar with these nonwords: "totla"; "itslef"; "poltical." Bernstein foregrounds a moment of the writing process almost universally repressed.

Such orthographic conflicts exist in modernism and later in New American poetry. On one side is Pound's ideology of accuracy, the Don'ts for Imagists and his passion for *le mot juste*; on the other is the romance of an oceanic, uncontrolled poetry as in Williams's "The Yachts," or *Spring and All* and *The Descent of Winter*.[6] A similar opposition can be found within Robert Duncan's work. Dropping a silent *e* can signify action against authority;[7] but at times distorted orthography signifies moral dysfunction. A catalog of defective U. S. Presidents begins: *"The Thundermakers descend,* / damerging a nuv. A nerb. / The present dented of the U / nighted stayd."[8]

Contrary to Williams and Duncan, Bernstein is insisting on antimastery in a self-contaminating way. He is not bending orthography to criticize wrongful power outside the poem or to signal his own elect status; rather, he is destroying any image of power within his own writing, abjuring the conventional tasks of the poet and rewards for the reader. The line breaks seem deliberately nonsignificant; and if we make the orthographic corrections, we get prose, casually disguised as verse.

A summary will show the poem's dual commitment to the cause of nonmastery and error. Bernstein opposes a rigid binary of nonsense and sense; he calls for unconventional forms that allow greater sense-making than does the dominant discourse, such as Bush's speeches, which make no sense because of their hyperconventionality. Nonsense may involve two sensible readings; sense may occur in the process of oscillation between aspects.

But such summarizing is false to the writing of the poem. My act enforces the regime of sense—its meaning is made by excluding non-sense; an abstracting, dominating operation. As the poem's images would have it, such summary language, rather than jeweler's tools, is a steamroller, crushing the peculiarities of linguistic, lettristic embodiment into a flat instrumentality.

Looked at in this light, "A Defence" becomes an attack on all evaluative judgments. The institutional implications are extreme: grades, awards, tenure, the canon could not exist in a regime where language was composed of singular, nonhierarchical marks—if such could be called a language: this would be the territory of a prime Derridean paradox where the repeatability of a word (its meaning) clashes with its unique existence as a physical instance. The domination of the governing discourse would be impossible, and we would have reached the utopia of the liberated signifier, the sagnifire, the snugifirm, teh nugiform.

But such a conclusion oversimplifies the institutional dynamics. Beneath its melted orthography the poem's syntax is clear enough, as are its proposed changes in reading. What was suggested in *A Poetics* is acted out here in an attack on ghettoized poetic expression insulated from intellectuality—the poem is nothing if not intellectual, wittily exemplifying its concepts. But in its obsessive misspelling it also seems to reinscribe poetry as that which cannot be contained by any normative practice.

The powers of normativity, however, are not easy to disperse or to dispense with. The question of nonsense as posed by the poem is crucial only to the reading regimes of the academy. It is there the poem poses its dual challenge as transgressive writing and paradigmatic reading. Lines near the end read, "Crucialy, the duck/rabitt exmaple is one / of the ambiguity of *aspects* and clearly / not a bprobelm of noneselnse: tjere are / two competing, completely sensible, / readings.," "Noneselnse" is both a negligible typo and a cutting-edge term with claims of exclusivity. Bernstein is using poetry to signify on theory, and theory to signify on poetry. His duck/rabitt can be spelled out as authoritative theorist/powerless poet—or for "powerless" should we read a more intellectually attractive construct such as "powerfree"?

The same tension animates the poem's politics. Bernstein's opposition to the tyranny of the dominant discourse is clear—Bush's speeches are given as the example. Presidential power, however, does not operate solely on the level of discourse—unless we expand the concept to include social practices in general. Books and Doonesbury strips quoting Bush verbatim reveal how random and deteriorated his actual speech was; but clearly these errata promise scant political liberation. And if the target that Bernstein is attacking is a mirage of convention, the utopian politics of liberated textuality are also cloudy.

Textuality and Group Voice

One can invoke "the politics of textuality," but how easily do textuality and politics go together without special pleading? Questions of multiculturalism and cultural literacy—not to mention basic literacy—and issues of hierarchy and pedagogy can make textuality seem like a subject for a more stable time and readership. The farther outside the academy we go, the more textuality seems irrelevant to the sound bites and images that make the culture overwhelmingly visual and oral.

The previous Defences of Poetry to which Bernstein alludes were written to secure poetry within literate landscapes. For Sydney, the opponent was Gosson, representing the gathering of the Puritan attack on figurative language. For Shelley, while he was answering Peacock's prediction of the eventual extinction of poetry, there was an enemy more familiar to poets today: indifference. Both Sydney and Shelley claim a central position for poetry, but for Sydney, there is both a canon—the classics, the Bible, & some contemporaries —and a specific social function of poetry—it is the best school for ethics and social finesse.

The width and vagueness of Shelley's claims reveal how socially incoherent the definition of poetry had become. Poetry for Shelley is ubiquitous and radically unspecifiable. It is foundational since poets are "the inventors of the arts of life," ranging from language to statuary to law;[9] but poetry has no formal or rhetorical particularity. There is no difference between poetry and prose; differences of person, time, and place do not obtain; the fact of being embodied on the page is unpoetic, finally: "Veil after veil may be undrawn, and the inmost naked beauty of the meaning never exposed" (513); and of course there is the famous comparison of "the mind in creation" to a fading coal, where Shelley avers that "when composition begins, inspiration is already on the decline" (517). Sydney can hold out specific rewards—esteem, pleasure; Shelley can only promise power that is total but undeliverable: "Poets are the unacknowledged legislators of the world" (522).

Shelley's refusal to delimit poetry, however, has turned out to have been a successful tactic. His nondefinition of poetry has, in a most Shelleyesque way, diffused itself throughout the Western literary sphere, where its very vagueness has defined poetry. The supreme importance of poetry and its mystical difference from ordinary language are two of the primary virtues used to promote poetry in a world increasingly indifferent to it, by poets as various as Arnold, Rimbaud, Stevens, and Pound.

Shelley does not emphasize writing as the primary problematic of poetry, but the elements of such an emphasis are there. Once you deny the importance of person, place, and time, and speak of veils being withdrawn without revealing the innermost meaning, you allow for a writing that is at odds with its own physical embodiment, a writing that could include the dissonances of Bernstein's "Defence." In fact, such dissonances, foregrounding their own incompleteness, might be considered in some sense normative.

It is suggestive to apply twentieth-century literary ethnography to Shelley's "Defence." If we substitute "oral composition" for "poetry," some contradictions sort themselves out. The Homeric bards would be "the inventors of the arts of life"; yet the act of writing poetry down would—to telescope centuries—turn a tribal centrality into an urban specialization. Speech, and the community it invokes, would be the glow fading on the page and turning to the coal of nonresponsive print. Speech remains, however, almost legislative in the midst of the legalisms of the written word.

How pertinent the divide between orality and literacy is in Shelley is open to question. But if we turn to a last comparison to illuminate Bernstein's work, the focus of the relevance will sharpen. The following is from Kamau Brathwaite's *X/Self*, a book-length poem that plays glimpses of a yet-to-be-transcribed oral Caribbean history off against a Western epic history that has written colonized experience out of its epic tradition. Brathwaite calls the medium he is trying to create "nation language":

Dear Mama

i writin you dis letter/wha?
guess what! pun a computer o/kay?
like i jine de mercantilists!

. . . .
if yu cyaan beat prospero
whistle?[10]

Bernstein's nonbinary struggle between sense and nonsense—poetry and theory—is externalized here in *X/Self* as a conflict between eurocentric Western values and a nascent Afro-Carib culture Brathwaite wants to articulate. While the political agenda may be clearer, the dynamics of the conflict are no less tangled than in Bernstein's case. The gap between Western canonic narrative and African/Caribbean voice is present at every letter, both in the pedagogic struggle the spelling encodes and in the fact that the vernacular is being transcribed via computer. The "*X*" and the "*Self*" of the title could be read as standing on either side of this gap: is nation-language to create a new Self or an X that is separate from the universalist Western self? Is the slash between them a mark of strife or amalgamation? These tensions are like those in Bernstein's title, which could easily be *a/poetics*.

The blended temporalities of the next few lines make for rapid ironies: "is not one a dem pensive tings like ibm nor bang & ovid / nor anyting glori. ous like dat! / but is one a de bess tings since cicero o / kay? / / it have key / board & / evva / / ting. like dat ole / remmington yu have pun top de war. drobe up there ketchin duss / / only dis one yu na ave to benn down over & out / off de mistake dem wid white liquid paper / . . . / wid dis ting so now / long before yu cud say jackie robb / inson r. t-d2 or shout / / quink / / dis obeah blox / get a whole whole para / graph write up &" (80–81). The computer seems to be one with Cicero and Ovid; it is also futuristic and is being used to reclaim the past; but technology can go stale quickly: what is more out of date than liquid paper?

How read the cultural overtones of the following figure? "dat indonesia fella in star / trick / where dem is wear dem permanent crease up grey / / flannel cost / umes like dem gettin ready to / jogg / but dem sittin down dere in such silence a rome / it not turn / in a hair pun dem wig/wam & / hack/in out hack/in out all sorta read /out & fall / out & garbage & ting from all part/icles a de gal. axy" (82). Does this validate the pluralism represented aboard the *Enterprise* of *Star Trek*—is the "indonesia fella" (Sulu?) a citizen of a multicultural utopia, or is he merely an exotic token, a grey flannel organization man in the boardroom of the universe, a jogger, a hacker, a Roman centurion? These anxious questions reflect back on Brathwaite's position.

His writing is not solely an allegiance to ethnic inflection as opposed to universal Arnoldian culture. Some of Brathwaite's resistance to Western Civilization takes place in the endemic typographic distortions. "dat ole / remmington yu have pun top de war. drobe" is an emblem of his creolization of the Western epic tradition: his language is a pun on top of a war.

In his notes at the end, Brathwaite agonizes as he finds himself almost in the position of an Eliot, supplying the poem with the authority of critical interpretation. In more normative prose Brathwaite writes that he provides the notes "with great reluctance, since . . . they may suggest the poetry . . . is bookish, academic, 'history'. Which therefore makes my magical realism, the dub riddims and nation language and calibanisms appear contradictory; *how could these things come from a learned treatise?*" (113). While Brathwaite's reaction to the academy as the enemy of poetry's immediacy is powerfully evident, his desire for a political efficacy is stronger—he does write the notes after all. The mediating academy, destroyer of magic though it may be, is a means to a wider common audience, one that would potentially exist on both sides of the slash in the book's title.

Writing and Power

Such disparate anti-orthographies finally may not end up as all that binary. First, I want to cite the last lines of Bernstein's poem, which, shockingly, are spelled perfectly (with the italics lending an almost Yeatsian sententiousness): "b6y the waylines 9–10 are based on an / aphorism by Karl Kraus: *the closer we / look at a word the greater the distance / from which it stares back.*" Kraus staring at a word, hypnotized by the auratic strangeness of print, the inexplicable arrangement of lines and curves of the letters, the delicate seraphs, the bizarreness of its silent call to sound—this is a reader for whom the language holds out the promise of endless significance. But such fixation on the letter connotes an empowered native speaker. A nonnative speaker would want to translate, get the message; the strangeness of the word would not be an uncanny revelation, it would be an all-too-familiar experience.

The following stanzas, from the "Dies Irie" of *X/Self*, display an opposite relation to Kraus's bemused position vis-à-vis power: they want it.

> Day of sulphur dreadful day
> when the world shall pass away
> so the priests and shamans say
>
> . . . .
>
> to what judgement meekly led
> my lai harlem wounded knee
> fedon fatah sun yat sen
>
> . . . .
>
> day of sulphur guernica
> when the world shall pass away
> so the priests and pundits che (37)

It would be easy enough simultaneously to award the palm to the revolutionary commitment of *X/Self* and to dismiss Bernstein's anarchy. I can imagine that a subtle, self-aware, and humorous Caliban makes a more attractive figure for many than a self-shattering "Hupty Dempty" (to recall the excerpt from "A Defence"), who seems to say little more than "Words can be spelled however I choose to spell them." Brathwaite's words exist in history, to the point where a revolutionary life becomes the embodiment of the verb of saying: "so the priests and pundits che." By extension, the act of writing *X/Self* can be seen as a parallel revolutionary act. Such a statement, however, requires a major caveat. "By extension" masks a problem: the idea of revolutionary writing is based on a revolutionary reading of it, which in turn is based on the academic security of intellectual flexibility. And Bernstein, despite his many gestures of renunciation, also wants power, at least in a more local academic arena: we should not forget that it is also Humpty/Hupty who says: "The question is—which is to be master, that's all." The poetry-as-error aspect of the poem suggests the answer is: no one (but to reiterate: the poetry-as-theory aspect is enmeshed in its own power struggles).

The Brathwaite lines just cited evoke the Last Judgment; as a whole *X/Self* ends with the return of Xango, who the notes tell us is the "Pan African god of thunder, lightning, electricity and its energy, sound systems, the locomotive engine and its music" (130). But while Brathwaite's poetry may reach toward the divine realm for its ultimate authority, this authority is mediated by the fallen realm of institutionalized reading, the audience addressed not only by the poem, but by the notes, which is where the definition of Xango occurs. The notes, even though tentative and contingent, are after all more final than—or at least placed after—the end of the poem and the return of the god.

Bernstein, both in *A Poetics* and in "A Defence of Poetry," tries to forestall any theological finale. The ever-receding word of Karl Kraus is the opposite of the Last Judgment; it flees from any definitive manifestation of The Word. This impulse suggests an opposing corollary to Coleridge's claims about the divinity of poetry. Coleridge considered the imagination as an echo of God's creation: "a repetition in the finite mind of the eternal act of creation in the infinite I AM."[11] That is from the writer's side; the theological equivalent for the reader would be an echo of the Last Judgment. This penultimate judgment is what, in Bernstein's model of writing, the writer continually avoids.

Critical models and writing practice are not often synonymous; and as a writer's career continues the differences often become pronounced. In his most recent work, Bernstein has been coming closer to making straightforward statements while allowing himself to be identified in a more straightforward way. Sections of "The Lives of the Toll Takers" (1994) seem, in places, almost like an aesthetic self-portrait. If we take "Jew" as the Jabèsianwriteras-Jew mentioned in *A Poetics*, then the following passage enacts Bernstein's version of nation language:

> The hidden language of the Jews: self-reproach, laden with ambivalence, not this or this either, seeing five sides to every issue, the old *pilpul* song and dance, obfuscation clowning as ingratiation, whose only motivation is never offend, criticize only with a discountable barb: Genocide is made of words like these, Pound laughing (with Nietzsche's gay laughter) all the way to the canon's bank spewing forth about the concrete value of gold, the "plain sense of the word", a people rooted in the land they sow, and cashing in on such verbal usury (language held hostage) . . .[12]

The multiple switches in aspect between self-portraiture, self-mockery, and severe condemnation of Pound's aesthetic illustrate the fact that "the duck/rabitt . . . ambiguity of *aspects*" need not be confined to a semantic level. "The hidden language of the Jews" could be taken from an anti-Semitic pamphlet; the "clowning as ingratiation" phrases are a sharp self-criticism of one basic mode of Bernstein's rhetoric; the tone of "spewing forth" indicates real rage against the hysterical callousness of Pound's racial pronouncements. Such dense clangor is serious.

For both Bernstein and Brathwaite, writing is an engine of social change. *X/Self* projects a global transformation; its altered textuality—nation-language—is not an already existing vernacular but is the flag of an emerging constituency. Bernstein's writing envisions individual enclaves of textual freedom standing in for politics. In neither case would Vendler's citation of Bishop's cry of readerly judgment, "Heavens, I recognize the place, I know it!" be possible: the "places" that the writing aims to enact do not yet exist—unless we consider that they have an initial, nonoriginary existence in a discursive arena that includes both poetry and criticism. In neither case, to return to the initial set of images, can the lecture hall and heaven be separated.

SIX

Building a More Powerful Vocabulary:
Bruce Andrews and the World (Trade Center)

Iconoclasm and Its Discontents

Not many days after the 1993 bombing of the World Trade Center, the *New York Times* ran an article discussing the structure of the building and the possibilities of its being brought down by a larger and more thoughtfully placed explosion. It turns out not to be easy: apparently, each tower is built to withstand the impact of a fully loaded jet liner taking off. In addition to the strength of the structure, attackers would have to confront its complexity: there are twenty-one load-bearing pillars and they could not be reached simultaneously by the force of an explosion. In being destroyed, a particular section would in fact shield other areas by absorbing the impact. The timing and placement of the article is interesting in itself: it was a rapid-response anodyne to the spiral of geopolitical urban trauma while at the same time, under the cover of a discussion of engineering, it invited its readers to participate in transgressive calculations of how the Trade Center towers might actually be brought down.

It is not easy to translate violence to paper convincingly. Literary revolutions may be hard to pull off on the page, but it is much harder to translate any of their energy from the page to the outside world. I am invoking the bombing here, however, to begin to consider the structure of the problem that Bruce Andrews has been confronting in his work over the last two decades and particularly in a recent book, *I Don't Have Any Paper So Shut Up (or, Social Romanticism)*. Andrews has been one of the more visible language writers, publishing over twenty chapbooks and books of poetry, and co-editing $L=A=N=G=U=A=G=E$ magazine with Charles Bernstein in the late seventies and early eighties as well as *The $L=A=N=G=U=A=G=E$ Book*.[1] In his criticism he has been insistent on the politicization of poetry, attacking conventional writing as the signature of laissez-faire politics; his poetry has been highly disjunct in syntax, semantics, and typography. *I Don't Have Any Paper* marks a significant change in his work: while it is still resolutely anticonventional, it ventures into the most charged and obvious areas of contemporary politics in easily legible and very aggressive ways. In *I Don't Have Any Paper* the bombs may be verbal and their targets metaphorical, but the scale and complexity of what Andrews is trying to bring down presents him with a conundrum whose social geometry is similar to the physical geometry that ultimately contains a bomb blast: whatever he destroys tends to shield contiguous and remote areas. Of course, this is all just a metaphor. Does "destroy" here simply resolve to "ironize"?

Before turning to *I Don't Have Any Paper*, I want to look at an article of Andrews's, "Constitution / Writing, Language, Politics, the Body," that provides a good summary of his intentions, constructive and destructive, for writing. I will also cite two passages from his earlier and subsequent poetry; these will demonstrate the difficulties of linking radical politics with radical poetics. The article makes clear that Andrews does not share my perception of these difficulties and that, for him, writing and politics are to be one thing. Such strong claims have given quite a charge to the reception of language writing. The strength of Andrews's claims on politics will not, however, rule out messy complications.

As is the case with any critique, the object of his dissatisfaction is in better focus than the kinds of activity he ultimately wants to see. He criticizes "conventional literature (the novel as exemplar)," whose goal, he says, "is clarity, transparency; the medium should go away, leave no trace," and instead be "a direct window on the world." This results in "a laissez-faire order, presided over by the invisible hand of language (as if it were hegemonic Great Britain in the nineteenth century.)" It leaves no room for change: "The world is already constituted, and that is that. Not **this**, but **that**" (155). Andrews asks, "If writing as an art activity is reduced to this, what are the political implications—the politics of this, and I don't mean literary politics." Writing, that is, does not have a separable literary politics. The politics of normative writing are, he writes, complacency; they "reinforce the sinews and consequences of the social world—its facticity, its thickness, its naturalness, its obviousness, its massiveness, its resistance to change" (156). There is a real question as to how reified Andrews's own dismissal of conventional literature is. After all, *Ryder*, *Midnight's Children*, and *The Bonfire of the Vanities* are all novels, but however direct or mediated a connection we might want to make between writing and politics, Djuna Barnes, Salman Rushdie, and Tom Wolfe would seem to represent very different political agendas. (Applied to certain areas of contemporary poetry, Andrews's critique of transparency seems to me more valid.)

Against the inertia of normativity he proposes "a structuralist anti-system poetics" (157) that would disrupt transparent reference. His call for disruption is itself disruptive:

> a poetics of subversion. nomenclature . . . / *dishevel* . *Tumult verbal* . *secular violation* . [. . . my ellipsis] *uses bad language* / *anarchy otherwise* . *non-signs* . To oppose the structural underpinnings by an antisystematic detonation—*dizzying* . . . *elasticize* . . . *by flashes* . . . non-signs . . . scrambled—by a blowing up of all settled relations. *sentence can dislocate* . *mangled matter*." (158–59)

Andrews recognizes the problem that his call for such subversion raises. By its processes of interchangeability, multinational capital has already produced a radical dislocation of particulars. Marx's "All that is solid melts into air" can in fact be read as saying that capitalism is constantly blowing up its own World Trade Centers in order to build newer ones. If this is true, then "to call for a heightening of these deterritorializing tendencies may risk a more **homogenizing** meaninglessness . . . an 'easy rider' on the flood tide of Capital" (159). This is a difficult position to avoid. As markets become saturated there is a steady demand for flashier items that are also firmly saleable. The processes of commodification are ubiquitous and can make the seque from Jackson Pollock to new Formica patterns seem as inevitable as the seasons.

In attempting to avoid such aesthetic innocuousness, Andrews pins his hopes on the body. It is not the site of identity or self-expression; rather, it is something of a utopian counterweight to the various registers of false rhetoric he feels surrounded by. He calls for a writing whose "reception is by bodies" (163); but this is not a writing which is "a blandly 'communicative' or 'expressive' act, for too often what is 'expressed' and 'communicated' is not the *doer position* but a previous social construction, of more and more dubious value" (162).[2]

Neither his earlier work nor a subsequent book, *Tizzy Boost*, are at all "blandly communicative"; the levels of disjunction are quite high.[3] Here are two small samples:

> let me see if I can remember
> staccato mildews outings be hooked illusory workplace obstreperous
> schizophrenia & 'free' to not interested in
> warmth I'm dreaming extra evince
> singers move the side effects but as yet lesbians of the hit
> cha   Effort sucks duty
> get up get into get involved
> sound politics peristaltic jockey crotch down how many

crawl manufactured in Hollywood male voices depiction obsolete
    ("I Guess Work the Time Up")[4]

The radius leaks back payments, we promise
two fingers
    clever fronting plus or minus
    as if surface could
              luxury confiding
              tongues fail with failure,
                    bacterial
              atonement ethics   by its sound
   (Tizzy Boost, section 19)[5]

It is difficult to assign excerpts any particular relation to any particular politics, especially excerpts like these. It might be possible to deduce from the vocabulary or from the syntactic rupture that Andrews's concerns are political. But it would be a fairly innocuous deduction, one that would be most likely to be made by those readers who are already prepared to grant such disjunct surfaces a politics; such readers would likely be those who know Andrews's poetry, his essays, and what he stands for. But for readers who are not familiar with Andrews the politics of such writing would probably be difficult to fathom. With *I Don't Have Any Paper*, on the other hand, the political dimension is much more obvious, and as a result the consequences are more obvious as well. It is a highly charged writing that bristles with problematic political statements at all points. But if *I Don't Have Any Paper* is so 'political' that all excerpts will show it clearly, to determine what Andrews's politics are in the book is another story. In my reading I want to keep in mind relations between two of Andrews's prior terms: "the *doer position*," implying a sense of social activism, and "a previous social construction," which I take to indicate inherited possibilities of identity. Between these two lies a large question: is the political agency of poetry in Andrews's project compatible with any assertion of identity?

In *I Don't Have Any Paper* maintaining the "*doer position*" requires a high dosage of transgression. Verbal violence is continuous, occurring almost word to word. It's as if "previous social constructions"—older identities, normative phrases—are threatening to coalesce every moment. I'll start with a small phrase: "cathartic cuckold in ballroom needs no Hitler" (230).[6] One could call this humor, politics, performative rhetoric, or poetry, but it can also be read as a series of explosions targeted at what Andrews perceives as the clear windows of normative writing and the promises of cultural value displayed behind those windows: "cathartic" is directed against notions of Aristotelian tragedy and, following from that, Arnoldianism, Great Books as the foundation of university curricula; "cuckold" attacks marriage, faithfulness, sacramental heterosexuality, the pathos of Leopold Bloom in *Ulysses*; "in ballroom" is aimed at Lawrence Welk, respectable bourgeois sublimation; "needs no Hitler" attacks, I think, political rhetorics that posit Hitler as the absolute of evil thus allowing us to look at the Hitler-less present as relatively safe and sane. This is a lot of cultural structure to try to explode. The fact that almost every phrase in the book continues such demolition indicates how hard it is to achieve the impact Andrews wants. A basic conundrum surfaces: don't such attacks tend to reinforce their target at least as much as they explode it? It is a perpetually reemerging presence, there in every phrase.

There is a great difference between reading the book and quoting a sentence from it; I don't know how my ventriloquy of Andrews's attacks will strike those who aren't familiar with his work. *I Don't Have Any Paper* is 250 pages long; each page is dense, and the sentences or lines (the typography is a hybrid of prose and verse) are complex. By itself, "cathartic cuckold in ballroom needs no Hitler" could be read with Hitler remaining a firm moral term: the cathartic cuckold won't fall prey to fascism. But if it is read in bulk, construing the book for such resolutions won't work:

> grub sits sharp — pull crabs from brainpan; the demolished call had Israeli
> diplomatic plates. Squint to think
> psychology becomes multinational; death to sin or sin to death semantic
> bluff. Jet jack
> video the dwarfs alone no wrongdoing by any judge — neural tune, pope's
> nose—to the swift completion of their appointed rounds—cathartic cuck-
> old in ballroom needs no Hitler.
> Maybe normal happiness is what I dread; treat all men with unspeakable
> contempt. (230)

Another 'fascism' passage reads as follows:

> I love these obvious things. Please, darling
> my knees are on Marx — and this is not indicative of what we most want
> — we should have gone to multi-themes! Make the corrections with your
> fist in the socket, the transformation of Africa into a plantation for the
> commercial hunting of black skins — diabetes. Brown & black sales pitch:
> the East is Red, milk makes you deposit. Poignant exile by screeching
> weekend Nazis, makeup for pets stupids wound; we're just the *units* of a
> self-reproductive system—we're part of the *methods*. (150)

I put scare quotes around 'fascism' because it seems that one of the goals of these passages is to neutralize the moral certainties around such words as "Nazis." Andrews's target is not some specific set of attitudes in the cultural and corporate Western world, but their sum: "psychology" has become "multinational"; the individual is "just a *unit* in a self-reproducing system." Andrews dreads, not just "normal happiness," but all laissez-faire acceptance of the boundaries of this unit.

Taste is one of the principal bulwarks against which the writing hurls itself. On every page there are phrases such as "Tear-gas the middle class. Blondes have more enemas." (171), or "why don't I just squeeze some of my pimple juice into your herpes scar?" (151) But grossness is just a subset of the larger desire for disruption of perceived systems of control. These include the largest social constructs (government, the law) as well as the details of these constructs (lawyers playing squash). But equally important targets for Andrews are the control-systems implanted within literacy: he is continually disrupting expectations for well-formed sentences, narrative, and consistent sequences of imagery:

> why don't I just squeeze some of my pimple juice into your herpes scar? Squash courts of the mind under penalty of law, total chaos! — yeah — cellular difficulty would sound great. Happy Pilgrim Trials to you! Slobs at the red bar — cataracts! Dog-doo government is corrupt cough control through colonization, crucifix, big wampum. You just have no respect for people as cultural artifacts; I just lost my U.N. seat. (151)

In such a corrosively ironic text, it is hard to take any phrase at face value; nevertheless I think it is safe to say that Andrews has no respect for people as cultural artifacts and that he is glad to have lost his U.N. seat. This signals a major divide between some multicultural and experimental writing, though great allowance must be made for nuances and outright exceptions. But—to make a stark comparison—when Andrews is compared with Maya Angelou a specific distinction will emerge.

Cultural and Aesthetic Identities

On most maps of poetry terrains, the distance between Andrews and Angelou makes for a very wide stretch, of course: their audiences, aesthetics, publishing networks, and levels of cultural visibility are vastly different. But the question of political identity will make for a common focus. For Andrews the boundaries of the individual present no obstacle to the penetration of global capital: the individual is just a unit of larger forces. Formal innovation becomes a primary site of resistance; any nostalgia for individuality is insidious. For Angelou, on the other hand, the boundaries of the individual are the site of contestation.

> There is a true yearning to respond to
> The singing River and the wise Rock.
> So say the Asian, the Hispanic, the Jew
> The African, the Native American, the Sioux,
> The Catholic, the Muslim, the French, the Greek,
> The Irish, the Rabbi, the Priest, the Sheikh,
> The Gay, the Straight, the Preacher,
> The Privileged, the Homeless, the Teacher.
> They hear. They all hear
> The speaking of the Tree.

There are many reasons why Andrews will not be invited to read at any foreseeable inauguration, but high on the list would be the intensity of his aggression toward the range of ethnic and cultural identities that Angelou's poem celebrates. The categories themselves and especially their aestheticization— Jew/Sioux; Greek/Sheikh; Teacher/Preacher—are primary targets of Andrews's writing. *I Don't Have Any Paper* was written before Clinton's inauguration; nevertheless, the following passage serves well as a hypothetical response to Angelou's multiculturalism and as an example of Andrews's anticulturalism: "We gave the Jews Israel so let's give Puerto Rico to the Palestinians & then have some Finlandization of Canada. Obvious algebraic suicide, am unopposed, squealch-a-roni platitudes as tinder box; would you prefer infantilization or pedestalization? Exception! Clean soot from punt" (189).

Andrews undoubtedly would define Angelou's poem as squealch-a-roni platitudes: a blandness that is ultimately a tinderbox. But what are his politics here, apart from critique? Does his writing take a position on the Palestinians, or French Quebec? If we take these sentences as discursive, and not as art, then they seem to say that nationalism is a dead end: "Obvious algebraic suicide." Identity politics, as I am reading this passage, offers poor alternatives. "Would you prefer infantilization or pedestalization?" I.e., Do you still beat your wife? Do you still read your Keats? But how read the politics of "Exception!"? Surely the individuality of American exceptionalism is exactly not what Andrews is touting. Not that we are supposed to treat any one sentence as the site of Andrews's position. But given the book's opposition to narrative and its insistent phrasal pulse, any one sentence or phrase becomes by default the recursive site of agency, whether political or literary. The passage retreats to a safe (pronounless) haven of exciting active sound, a kind of *Klangfarbenmelodie*: "clean soot from punt."

These last four words may remind some readers—they do me—of the percussive abstraction of Clark Coolidge's work. I want to turn briefly to a recent poem by Coolidge and Larry Fagin, because it will shed light from a different angle on the troubling political terrain surrounding the intersection of formal experiment and identity poetics. It will also demonstrate that the tensions in *I Don't Have Any Paper* are not simply the result of a personal gripe.

Coolidge and Fagin parodied Angelou's inaugural poem by using an OULIPO method of defamiliarization. Every noun Angelou used was replaced by a noun seven words removed in the dictionary. Thus the passage I quoted earlier becomes:

> There is a true yawn to respond to
> The singing Roach and the wise Rock Crystal.
> So say the Ash Can, the Hippogriff, the Jetsam,
> The Afterbirth, the Native American Legion, the Sinner,
> The Catnip, the Musskellunge, the Freezer, the Great White Way,
> The Ipso Facto, the Quota, the Prima Donna, the Sheet,
> The Gavel, the Stovepipe, the Prawn,
> The Prism, the Homburg, the Taxi.
> They hear. They all hear
> The spatter of the Tree of Heaven.[7]

If Andrews is playing with fire in a decentered, all-over fashion, Coolidge and Fagin are, with these substitutions, picking up specific burning brands one after the other. Some of the changes are particularly charged: Asian - Ash Can; Native American - Native American Legion; Rabbi - Quota, etc. To any identifying reader these substitutions might feel like insulting jokes. But if one tried to ascribe a particular location to the source of the insult, it wouldn't be easy. This isn't Andrew Dice Clay joking about faggots, or a racist attack. It is the dictionary's random speech. If we allow ourselves the double vision that the parody assumes, the oddness of the results can be funny. The alphabetic proximity of "Catholic" to "Catnip" or of "Gay" to "Gavel" furnishes a compact display of the arbitrariness of language. And then there is a second level, on which the arbitrary suddenly becomes paradoxically meaningful. Being gay will mean, for the next few decades, dealing with courtrooms and gavels directly or indirectly; "stovepipe" is a surprisingly good nickname for "straight," both geometrically and with its New England crackerbarrel connotations.

But we should not lose sight of the basic fuel of the parody, which is a great dissatisfaction with the coalition of identities that Angelou is positing, and the emphatic rejection of its rhetoric that works with established cadences and symbols, not single words. I imagine that it was the specific inclusiveness of

Angelou's poem, plus its being officially recognized as poetry by an incoming administration, that triggered the desire to pull the rug from under it. I doubt that it would have seemed like a particularly good idea to redo, say, Amiri Baraka's "It's Nation Time." But for all of its vocabularistic satire on names and specific identities, the subject position from which "On the Pumice of Morons" is funny is itself specific: it is one where all resources of language are present and equally available; the writer must be able to take possession of all the words in the dictionary without any moments of alienation. There is one restriction involved, however: all particular identification has to be eliminated. Any investment in present tense collectivities—or to put it another way, any present tense political identity—is banished. To parody Angelou is to reject a unification of poetry and politics of a far different kind than Andrews calls for. But if political poetry is defined as having an effect beyond the purely literary sphere, then Angelou's unification has a much stronger grip on the title than Andrews's aggressiveness. Rock, river, and tree used as large symbols may grate on a spectrum of poetic sensibilities, but as political speech their vacuousness can be seen as strategic and as forming vehicles for more specific messages. She used her momentary political capital to recite a rhythmic call for a multicultural coalition with antimilitarist overtones. How much efficacy we want to grant these overtones is a question.

Directly opposing such inclusiveness, Andrews trashes any autonomy of social parts based on race, class, gender, or sex: "Why should he like guys?— he's no lesbian" (276); "Synapses hate grooves, they hate them = social relations are overrated. My mind . . . is not here today; when did the liberals run out of your money? Defoliated hopes of the branding iron, all ethnicity is a virus; irony is for squares" (194). Yet the consistent dismissal of identity does not alter the fact that Andrews is writing in a world that is as least as striated and segmented as Angelou's. It is hard to read for many lines without encountering markers of race, class, gender, or sex. But they are uniformly bent. Even though "irony is for squares," it is also Andrews's primary mode. (Note how even the outmoded "squares" is ironic.) A sentence such as "I'm deeply worried about the rapid pace of Israeli colonization of the West Bank" (162), while very probably true enough if we read the "I" as referring to the person of Bruce Andrews, comes off as one of the more ironic in the book. A much more "normal" utterance of the author-position would be: "Why did the Israelis let the Christian militia into the camps? — to impress Jodie Foster" (159).

Bruce Andrews, the person, is in evidence in spots throughout the book. There are moments of wry-to-dour literary politics that can only be construed as personal: "I don't allow anyone to rewrite what I write; on the other hand, no one wants to read it" (175–76); "this is a conspicuously *ignored* avant-garde, that's for sure" (175); "This is not so-called language writing" (64). One small passage is straight autobiography. Despite Andrews's hostility to narrative, the following, with its temporal structure of writer looking back down the path that led to the present moment of writing, could almost be called a *Bildungsroman*—a short one, to be sure: "My graduate education, most of which I devoted to thinking about neo-marxist theories of advanced capitalism and imperialism, was entirely financed by a grant, awarded under the National Defense Education Act, NDEA, which was passed in 1958, in reaction to the Soviet Union's triumphant launch of Sputnik in 1957, putting a satellite in space ahead of the U.S. So: thank you, Nikita!" (180). But such moments allowing a reader to narrativize the person writing are anomalous. There is another dimension, however, where the writer is constantly present: the activity of Andrews's cultural aggression is impossible to ignore.

Global capital, the ultimate target, is unlocalizable and can never be hit. This means that Andrews attacks the proximate target, the autonomy of the self, all the more fiercely. Breaking the individual from a unity into a unit is what is at stake when Andrews speaks of "making the corrections" with his "fist in the socket." This last phrase has at least two opposed readings. Either the writer is jamming his hand in where the lightbulb should go, in which case the aggressiveness is aimed inward, with the writer short-circuiting himself, or "the socket" is someone else's, say, the reader's eye socket. I find this double or split meaning symptomatic of a schism in his attitudes toward violence.

Literary Violence

Andrews flirts heavily with registers of violence throughout the book, from the title onward. There is a continual intent to shock: for instance, the suggestion above to "transform Africa into a plantation for the commercial hunting of black skins." One could cull unleashed attack-phrases from just about any page: "Sharon Tate is not worth the math" (308); "Africans would just be Caucasians in heat" (223); "*sink* the boat people!" (102); "You know, kill the red man & you've got yourself a homeland, bro—it's called the little homeland concept" (302); "why don't you just tie a mattress to your back?" (291). Such phrases attack whatever cultural identity is immediately in front of them, but Andrews denies that these are his words; he is not expressing himself: "Don't write down your thoughts; libido rests on laurels / difference engine— I'm just a trashy slow bitch; we haven't even been to this fucking wing yet" (75). Rather than trying to join the center and make it more various, he is carrying out Lyotard's archetypal command to postmodern intellectuals to "wage a war on totality."[8] Andrews's version of the slogan might be *"Connections are wrong"* (162).

To recall my earlier question—and Andrews's earlier worry—how can such a slogan be firmly separated from the homogenizing power of "the flood-tide of capital"? *"Connections are wrong"* is not, at least in logical space, so very far from Adam Smith's fear of "combination," i.e., from union busting. But of course this is an absurd conclusion to apply to a writer of Andrews's leftist convictions. To quote from his criticism again: "writing . . . can **charge** material with possibilities of meaning—not by demolishing relations but by creating them, no holds barred, among units of language" ("Constitution," 164).

Reading through *I Don't Have Any Paper* makes it hard to put much credence in Andrews's interest in creating relations. Rather, "charge" becomes the key word. After a few pages, it is difficult not to read for hot spots—passages which are also more syntactically normative:

> Oh glaze me big! Bribe on the mend.
> Get a million dollars of business advice —for a million dollars; chew gum til dream passes: perfect ear is no alarm.
> Crime teething hero God inhibits us all indifferently—especially you!, adumbrates—so thin, so light, so crisp;
> fur stops a drain
> as Jesus taught, excuse my parole. Where's a battered woman—I want to beat her up? Control the budget & you have them by the predestined — spectacle of double digit organs, blue violet with a hole in its middle. "One" cleans up the act. (193)

For me, at any rate, the sentence about the battered woman stands out. How much credence are we supposed to put in that question mark? The rhetoric is indecisive. It's not "I want to beat up a battered woman" (which would be like Baudelaire's "Let's Beat Up the Poor"), but neither is it "Can we possibly understand the twisted feelings of someone who wants to beat up a battered woman?" It's hard to imagine Andrews is condoning abusive men, but what, besides triggering a conflicted response, does such a sentence do? In spite of my initial discussion of Andrews's critique of catharsis, is *I Don't Have Any Paper* to be read as simply *cathartic*, as a kind of megaphone for the political unconscious? Even though Andrews, unlike the bourgeois artist, avoids all hint of narrative or imagistic resolution, such a commitment to catharsis would bring him quite close to the essence of aesthetic appeal. Wouldn't that make the book art, in the separated liberal sense that Andrews attacks, and not politics?

Such neo-Kantian enclaves have made attractive retreats in earlier cases. Andrews is nowhere as violent or virulent as Céline, and of course has not got into the kind of peril that made Céline, after being jailed for collaborating with the Nazis during World War Two and for writing his anti-Semitic pamphlets, take refuge in the neutral identity of artist. Andrews's frames of reference are more pulverized, but Céline's tone is not all that dissimilar: "[The Church is the] most shameless gambling joint for corn-holed Christianese the kikes have ever laid hands on."9 Beyond the tone, though, there is a glaring difference. When Andrews writes, "*sink* the boat people," he doesn't mean it—and thus finally could be said to write under the aegis of a Kantian disinterestedness, even though that leads to a liberal poetics of free play. On the other hand, when Céline wrote a phrase that became notorious, "Je vous Zay," punning on the French for "I hate you" ("Je vous hais"), his readers seem to have included a gang of fascist collaborators who later murdered Jean Zay, the Jewish Minister of Education targeted by the pun. Whether Céline meant it or not, they did, carrying an interested reading to its deadly conclusion. After the war and his own time in prison, Céline attempted to resuscitate his career. In *Conversations with Professor Y*, a fictionalized discussion of his work, his boast about "the magic, the sorcery . . . the violence also" of his writing was fragile."10 Certainly "violence," when ensconced in an aesthetic context, is a positive code-word for heroism: replays of the painterly violence of Pollock are now banal commodifications. Andrews acknowledges this problem in places. Would "I want educated oxen; hey, fuckhead, this is art" (153) be the positive, and "I limited my rebellion to mere gestures in the guidebook" (167) be the negative of Andrews's ironized allegiance to art as the master frame? Either way, we should remember the situation in which he is writing. The wartime Céline published on the front pages of Vichy newspapers; Andrews is publishing in small-press books and magazines: what prestige they have is literary.

The title, *I Don't Have Any Paper So Shut Up (or, Social Romanticism)*, suggests that speech, not art, is Andrews's liberatory goal. The only organizing principle of the one hundred sections of the book is that they are arranged by title, alphabetically. Andrews doesn't "have any paper" in that he does not believe in the complexities of deferral that paper embodies. The constant insults, exclamations, and twists of common phrase, while they attack all images of subjectivity, are finally repeated assertions that the "*doer position*" is a vocal subject, that the doer is supposed to exist on the street, not the page. Is there a collectivity, present or future, this doer speaks for, or is the book an individual effort? Recall Andrews's call to "**charge** material . . . by [creating] relations . . . among units of language." Andrews emphasizes "charge"; but to me "units" seems finally more significant. If language is made up of units, broken apart as all things are by capitalism, and if nothing new is created beyond the horizon of the phrase or the sentence, then these new, charged units would still depend on capital for energy to band together in momentary transgression. The World Trade Center, in all its reified "facticity, thickness, naturalness, obviousness, massiveness, resistance to change," would be a necessary malefic magnet. To avoid this conclusion I think it is necessary to posit a writer whose actions do not take place in the present political land-scape, a writer for whom the aesthetic sphere formed an autonomous space. Within this space, however, the notion of political art would be a metaphor if not an oxymoron.

Andrews's politics in *I Don't Have Any Paper* are either literary or improb-able. But I do not want to conclude by simply rejecting Andrews's project. While Andrews's attack on all identity (except that of writer-as-demystifier-of-all-subject-positions) leaves only a narrow margin for readers, nevertheless, the harshness of his attempts to write beyond race, class, and gender should not endorse a retreat to more normative genres and content. The political impossibilities of the present are impossible to escape. They still surround and in fact constitute the kindest sonnets, the most coherent reminiscences, the most spontaneous bop prosodies, the deepest metacritiques of signification, the most admirable ethical lessons.

SEVEN

This Page Is My Page, This Page Is Your Page: Gender and Mapping

Self and Map

The lyric "I" of the voice poem was a prime object of attack in early language writing theory and practice. But while the self as a final term of value in poetry was harshly disdained, the goal was not the avoidance of self demonstrated in the chance-generated work of John Cage and Jackson Mac Low or the Buddhist-inflected dissolution of the ego recommended at times by Gary Snyder, Jack Kerouac, and Philip Whalen. Language writers' attacks on the self were intermixed with desires to construct or enact some sort of person in poetry who would be of political consequence. The Vietnam War was the context. In an early talk, Barrett Watten aired his "personal gripe against 'the self'"; he set the modernist belief that it was "possible to make a world in which one would want to live" against the then-contemporary poetry scene, which he characterized as dominated by "the subjective aesthetic *bulge* . . . that seems useless and unreliable."[1] But at about the same time he began a book with these insistent lines:

> Could we have those trees cleared out of the way?
> And the houses, volcanoes, empires? The natural
> panorama is false, the shadows it casts are so many
> useless platitudes. . . .
>   . . . Admit
> that your studies are over. Limit yourself to your
> memoirs. Identity is only natural. Now become
> the person in your life. Start writing autobiography.[2]

Granted, the message here is conflicted: there is no "I" in the poem, only an imperiousness addressing a hectored "you"; the "natural panorama" is rejected in the first stanza whereas "natural" identity is valorized in the second; to "limit yourself to your memoirs" implies life is in the past, while to "become the person in your life" targets the future; the title of the poem is "Mode

Z," suggesting that becoming a person is something of an outlandish option to be tried after all the others have failed. Despite all these qualifications, however, the rhetoric of the final sentences is blunt enough to constitute a command that is not ironic.

This conflict around identity is political, though preceding chapters have foregrounded my suspicions about any automatic linkage on the formal level between poetics and politics. But the very weakness of the links between poet, community, and state makes the issues of power and place in society vital for the poet. The fact that poets are hardly on the map adds an intense twist to the questions, what kinds of maps are poems? What authority does the poet have as mapmaker? These questions can also serve in critical mapping. It is increasingly important to begin to establish linkages between differing sectors of the poetry world.

The relation between self and the surrounding space that poets claim in their poems is elemental in American writing, going back well beyond Whitman and Dickinson, where it surfaces powerfully. In England the landscape poem developed as a response to the phenomenon of enclosure: either as a pre-Romantic landscape with labor tucked away as picturesque smoke on the horizon; or as a Romantic vista where the poet's claims to socially important knowledge could be enacted without hindrance.[3] In America the historical crux was manifest destiny. Here I will go back only to the years immediately before language writing, and only look at a few writers; in the first part of the chapter these will be male: throughout, gender will be a crucial issue. I'll start with the moment of Robert Frost reciting "The Gift Outright" at Kennedy's inauguration. It may seem somewhat odd to devote attention to such a chestnut, but the poem foreshadows the Vietnam War and displays the paradigm for the poetics of accommodation by which a number of American poets ignored the war. It also shows how the male gaze is connected with the act of naming and possessing historical space. While such acts of possession would be attacked by language writers, they are difficult to avoid. It would be hard to imagine a poet less like Frost than Watten, but his questions, "Could we have those trees cleared out of the way? / And the houses, volcanoes, empires?" demonstrate, with sardonic negativity, the panoramic emptying that Frost's poem enacts. To participate in cultural battles one has to become a mapmaker or rely, however ironically, on older maps. Despite such postmodern assertions as Baudrillard's "The territory no longer precedes the map . . . it is the map that precedes the territory," prior poetic regimes and current social and material conditions confront the writer in every word.[4]

Charles Olson's notion of "COMPOSITION BY FIELD" is of course a key prior term.[5] However, the trajectory of Olson's later work and the work of

Robert Duncan and Jack Spicer, which I discuss briefly later in the chapter, grant an efficacy to poetic practice that has the effect of rendering the work less social, and the FIELD more vatic. I am interested here in seeing how writing is affected by its use of contemporaneous social language. Not COMPOSITION BY FIELD, then; more like, composition in the field of other users of language.

The Owner's Map

Frost's recitation was the high-water mark of cultural prestige for poetry in America. An anthology note captures some of the ideological nuances of the figure of the unified poet speaking to and for the unified nation: "by the time of his death in 1963, he was America's best-known poet. Millions of people had watched the windswept New England sage recite a poem at John F. Kennedy's televised presidential inauguration in 1961. . . . Writing in forms based on iambic lines and colloquial speech patterns, he positioned himself against both nothingness and the free verse experiments of modernists such as Ezra Pound and T. S. Eliot."[6] The moment was rich in symbols that continue to have relevance to contemporary poetry. There was the aged poet, embodying the commonsense anticosmopolitan values of Americana to such an extent that the anthology would describe him as if he were the landscape itself: "windswept." There was the specific pathos of the eighty-six-year-old blinded by the noon glare on his typescript with the youthful president trying ineffectually to provide shade for the page with his top hat. There was the very effective moment of performance when Frost gave up on the physical and intellectual distances involved in reading off a page and gazed out at the nation and recited, directly from his body as it were, "The Gift Outright," a poem which also insisted on a mystic connection between body and world: "The land was ours before we were the land's."

These simple words are eminently tricky: Frost is celebrating manifest destiny, but history is kept in decidedly soft focus:

> She was our land more than a hundred years
> Before we were her people. She was ours
> In Massachusetts, in Virginia,
> But we were still England's, still colonials,
> Possessing what we still were unpossessed by

After this beginning, political and historic specifics fade into even more elemental arrangements. Questions of who, at different times, lived on the land and named it are sidestepped. Jerome McGann notes this evasion: the Native

American name Massachusetts "reminds us that this supremely Anglo-American poem cannot escape or erase a history that stands beyond its white myth of Manifest Destiny"; Massachusetts reveals Virginia as a "lying, European word."[7] There are no more proper names after the three mentioned above; the rhetoric subsides into general considerations of ownership. The land becomes a woman, making us a corporate male that needs to make her ours; and the passage of historical time gives way to the drama of sexualized geopolitical possession with only a before and an after. Strength is crucially at issue in this Oedipal question, but it masked by a rhetoric of religious self-sacrifice:

> Something we were withholding made us weak
> Until we found out that it was ourselves
> We were withholding . . .
> . . . [we] found salvation in surrender.
> Such as we were we gave ourselves outright

"Giving ourselves" can be understood innocently as knowing a place well, clearing forests and cultivating farms. The land that is rhetorically the recipient of our gift and in reality the object of our possession is kept quite general and thus, beyond the poem, has room for many adherents from John Wayne in *Red River* to current ecological sensibilities expressed by poets such as Wendell Berry.

But the next lines reveal the limitations of the capacious optimism of the poem:

> we gave ourselves outright
> (The deed of gift was many deeds of war)
> To the land vaguely realizing westward.

The play on "deed of gift" / "deeds of war" does not exclude any war from the single act of giving ourselves to and taking possession of America; but the fact that war is the crucial act does exclude women from the large "we" the poem invokes. The mention of war only in parentheses and the cloudy uplift of the language keep particulars at bay; but "westward," even if it's qualified by "vaguely realizing," is still specific enough to implicate the Indian wars. If the 1942 publication date of the poem is kept in mind, "westward" stretches to— or at least gestures toward—the Pacific Theater of the Second World War.

If the date of the inaugural recitation is kept in mind, then the meaning of the poem can stretch still further to foreshadow the Vietnam War. Clearly, such a reference is foreign to the poem as a specific act of writing that took place in 1942, but the poem's own prophetic-colloquial invocation of manifest destiny invites such expansion. Such vague but compelling terms as "us" and "land" were central to the rhetoric under which the war was conducted, as "we" "fought for freedom," wherever it was deemed necessary by the war managers, trying to win "hearts and minds": in this context "vaguely realizing westward" points directly at South Vietnam. Of course, Robert Frost was not Robert McNamara or General Westmoreland. As a political act, his recitation was a minor ornament. But in terms of the explicit or subterranean political allegiances of poetry, Frost's position—lone sage facing and possessing the landscape for the nation—is an affirmation of the American status quo that is difficult for poets to ignore.

On the affirmative side, there would be figures such as William Stafford, whose "Travelling Through the Dark" opens Donald Hall's anthology *Contemporary American Poetry*. The poem narrates the moments after Stafford discovers a dead but still pregnant deer lying in the middle of the road. The deer is an immediate problem for other motorists—"that road is narrow—to swerve might make more dead."[8] But the end of the poem shows that the issue involves more than traffic:

> I stood in the glare of the warm exhaust turning red;
> around our group I could hear the wilderness listen.
>
> I thought hard for us all—my only swerving—
> then pushed her over the edge into the river.

Poems like this have often been attacked by language writers;[9] it is not the narrative content—in strictly local terms Stafford has done a good deed, after all, by clearing the road—but the historical rhetoric that is so problematic. There has been some damage to the land: the dead deer and the poet's angst are evidence. But the poem is not involved in a real debate about it. Making the climax of the poem the poet's thought seconded by the silent listening of the wilderness is to dramatize a foregone decision. (The scenario also dramatizes the fact that "voice" suppresses dialogue.) Stafford reports that he "thinks hard" but he writes an easily consumable pathos, invoking a community of isolated drivers—"us all"—none of whom can "swerve" from the way things are "vaguely realizing westward."

Frost's landscape is empty: "The Gift Outright" may memorialize the sacrifice made by fallen soldiers, but the invocation of manifest destiny also implies that America was an outright gift that did not displace anybody. Stafford improves upon Frost's history by acknowledging a victim of Western progress: the pregnant deer serves in a distant way to indicate aboriginal communities and women.[10] In many poems deriving from Frost's stance, there is no obstacle to the poet's possession of the landscape, except perhaps for some plants. This emptiness fills with individuality—which is not a neutral development. Reviewing *The Morrow Anthology of Younger American Poets*, Rae Armantrout pointed out that the editors' claims for the individuality of their poets masked a generalizing agenda. The editors' composite portrait of the anthologized poets turned out to have only one feature: "the younger poet tends to be himself, an invented version of himself." Such an insistence on individuality, which is often translated into the aesthetic necessity of "finding your voice," masks the institutional circuits, the network of presses, reviews, jobs, readings, and awards that are the actual sounding board of "voice." Politically, a crucial corollary to this uniqueness is an antipathy to explicit collectivity: the *Morrow* younger poet "is rarely a card-carrying group member, political or aesthetic." The editors may have intended poetry as an enclave of privacy, but their own celebration was inadvertently political, as the McCarthyite "card-carrying" suggests.[11] (Despite its invocation of "us," there is also an anticollective stance in the Stafford poem. "Around our group I could hear the wilderness listen" names only one person in "our group," which consists of "I," the car, and the dead pregnant deer.)

Discussing the *Morrow* anthology, Armantrout delineated what could be called the Sharp-Implement School. She noted the uniformity of the poems, and how they typically show the "younger American poet . . . outdoors in an 'abandoned' location doing physical labor with a sharp implement": e.g., "Picking grapes alone in the late autumn sun / A slight curving knife in my hand" (Poem A); or "I clear it with clippers; / slicing the prickly stalks / and tossing wiry tangles / of briars over the wall / to the cows" (Poem B).[12] This empowered, divisive male alone in the landscape fits snugly into the imperial flow of "the land realizing vaguely westward": his being alone helps that vagueness hold sway.

Others' Maps: Ginsberg and Ashbery

Such a male gaze and presence reinforces a generalized status quo while mining a static landscape for unchangeable emotion. While this has been a template for many poems, numerous counter-examples can be set against it. Of the few I will simply mention here, a major one would be Charles Olson. He is very much a male in a landscape, but the extensive particularity of his mapping of Gloucester contrasts strongly with the typicality that his fellow New Englander, Frost, aspires to. Robert Duncan's "fields" and "meadows"[13] oppose the naturalized consensus by turning inward to an intense imaginative existence on the page.[14] The territory that Jack Spicer's writing claims falls somewhere amid the linguistic field and the extraterrestrial (depending on the degree to which his references to taking dictation from "Martians" are taken metaphorically.)[15] Lines like the following, from different poems, make a polar opposition to "The Gift Outright":

> This ocean, humiliating in its disguises
> Tougher than anything.
> No one listens to poetry. The ocean
> Does not mean to be listened to.
>
> —
>
> I can't stand to see them shimmering in the impossible music of the
>   Star Spangled Banner . . .
>   The poetry
> Of the absurd comes through San Francisco television. Directly
>   connected with moon-rockets.
> If this is dictation, it is driving me
> Me wild.[16]

Rather than a landscape obedient to poetry, an apoetic ocean; rather than the authorative poet naming America, the poet shot to the moon by alienation when the national anthem plays on television. But in lieu of a detailed survey of the territory between Frost and language writing, I will compare two poems written during the Vietnam War: Allen Ginsberg's "Wichita Vortex Sutra" and John Ashbery's "Daffy Duck in Hollywood." In a number of ways, both poets are important precursors to language writing.

Ginsberg is a conscious heir of modernism, and the sense that accurate language and moral virtue are of a piece is basic to his work. Pound's slogan, "man standing by his word," is quoted in the poem, and Ginsberg draws a continuous analogy between evil politicians, their duplicitous language, and the horrible results. Headlines like *Rusk Says Toughness Essential For Peace* and *Vietnam War Brings Prosperity* are quoted for their Orwellian overtones; Johnson's claim that "We will negotiate anywhere anytime" is immediately followed by an Associated Press dispatch detailing U.S. reassurances to worried Thai rulers that the U.S. will not negotiate with the Viet Cong. But though "The war is language / language abused,"[17] it is finally not verbal clarity that Ginsberg poses against the war makers. "Accurate language" makes a noble enough slogan. But the poem dramatizes the troubling question: accurate to what?

The immediate answer is the landscape and the body. Ginsberg insists on the truth of the body throughout the poem, but it will turn out to be impossible to make this truth effective without resorting to the media, which are often

depicted as the demonic agents of distortion. This difficulty exists at the most
elemental level: the poem was spoken into a tape recorder while Ginsberg was
driving across Nebraska and Kansas;[18] the body and a duplicating medium
were both agents of its creation.

The poem begins as physical reportage, in Williams-esque registration of
landscape:

> Turn Right Next Corner
> *The Biggest Little Town in Kansas*
> *Macpherson*
> Red sun setting flat plains west streaked
> with gauzy veils, chimney mist spread
> around christmas-tree-bulbed refineries (110)

But the social dimension of Williams's "no ideas but in things" is not suffi-
cient for Ginsberg's purposes. When Williams writes poems such as "Fine
Work in Pitch and Copper," which ends, "One still chewing / picks up a copper strip / and runs his eye along it,"[19] he is equating the copper strip with his
own poetic line; and he is thus claiming as unambiguous a social status for
poet as for roofer. The poem is his union card. But for Ginsberg, who is
striving for immediate political effect, the world of things and people offers no
reassurance for his own identity as a poet. Throughout most of the poem,
Ginsberg is not comfortable with the stark physical and social landscape of
Kansas and the plain diction with which he tries to match it. Immediately after
the opening, he switches to the vatic mode:

> Kansas! Kansas! Shuddering at last!
> PERSON appearing in Kansas!
> angry telephone calls to the University
> Police dumbfounded leaning on
> their radiocar hoods
> While Poets chant to Allah in the roadhouse Showboat! (110)

Using his capitalized PERSON as a pivot, Ginsberg moves into the sonic
world, validated by the body: "Thy sins are forgiven, Wichita! / . . . . Come,
Nebraska, sing & dance with me— / Come, lovers of Lincoln and Omaha, /
hear my soft voice at last" (111). But as the wide geographical range of address indicates, Ginsberg's "soft voice" is not a perfectly local phenomenon.
The landscape is thoroughly enmeshed with media—"Iron interlaced upon the
city plain— / Telegraph wires strung from city to city O Melville!" (110–11).
In this magic realm, language realizes itself instantaneously. Ginsberg, Johnson, and Rusk become shaman-poets equally, battling it out in the broadcast

ether. The anticommunists are "bum magicians" using "Black Magic language" to present "World's Largest Camp Comedy: / Magic in Vietnam"; Ginsberg will invoke the positive magic of poetry. He wants the war to cease being a media event: "screaming faces made of dots / electric dots on Television," "Napalm and black clouds emerging in newsprint" (118–21). The war makers are "Sorcerer's Apprentices who lost control / of the simplest broomstick in the world: / Language" (120). He then calls on the "longhaired magician" to restore control. If we remember the scene from *Fantasia* the figure of the magician with the large, ancient book of spells under his arm and the robe and cap decorated with cosmological symbols will turn out to be quite well suited to play the part of the bard, reducing the spurious multiplicity of automatized broomsticks back to original simplicity. But what would that truth be in Ginsberg's poem? The alienating landscape? The return to singularity in *Fantasia* results from a theatrical sweep of the bard's phallocratic wand. The poem grants language a magical instrumentality, superseding its initial model of an undistorted language in a blank landscape. All language becomes spells.[20]

Ginsberg pronounces his "American Mantra": "I here declare the end of the War," aiming to take performative power away from the government. This is to grant himself full political agency. But he also wants the mantra to work. It does, briefly, but only in "language," i.e., in the media. Immediately after his pronouncement he sees the headline "*Kennedy Urges Cong Get Chair in Negotiations*" and comments, "The War is gone, / Language emerging on the motel news stand, / the right magic / Formula, the language known / in the back of the mind before, now in black print daily consciousness" (127–29).

A model of history that centers events in the speaking subject runs into problems rather quickly, especially in a poem which is also committed to registering news reports. The war comes back: 256 Vietcong are killed in a firefight. Ginsberg has to fall back on irony, with "language" now becoming a mantra that functions as critique not as a motor of change:

> Some of the
>   Language language
>   Communist
>   Language language soldiers
> charged so desperately
>   they were struck with six or seven bullets before they fell
>   Language Language M 60 Machine Guns
>   Language language in La Drang Valley
>   the terrain is rougher infested with leeches and scorpions
>   The war was over several hours ago! (129)

Ginsberg's desire to change the world by language has become trapped in the realm of language. But behind all images, Ginsberg posits an ultimate bastion of truth: the body. "Truth breaks through! / How big is the prick of the President? / . . . . / How big are all the Public Figures? / What kind of flesh hangs, hidden behind their Images?" (112). All history emanates from an acceptance or a distortion of "our Being, like a sunny rose / all red with naked joy" (125). But this universalism narrows slightly at the end of the poem, where Ginsberg traces the war back to the puritanical Carry Nation, who "by her violence / began a vortex of hatred that defoliated the Mekong Delta" (131–32). In an extension that is not all that surprising, the force of this bad national mother engulfs the poet's own mother, also a victim of this vortex:

> who died of the communist anticommunist psychosis
> in the madhouse one decade ago
> complaining about wires of masscommunication in her head
> and phantom political voices in the air (132)

Ginsberg himself has been hearing nothing but those phantom (media) political voices throughout the poem. By battling them to a standstill, he has in fact "ended the War," if not in the world at large, then in his own life at least: he has come to terms with the specter of his mother, accepted his own sexuality, and declared his body fully political.

There is a direct link in Ginsberg's poem between private and public: one person in a car, a single body speaking is asserted to be able to enter history, to sexualize, clarify, and alter it. Ashbery's writing, on the other hand, uses public materials casually and unpredictably. The contemporary world is visible, but the manner in which it touches any individual is hard to pin down. "Daffy Duck in Hollywood" provides an exemplary display of these difficulties.[21] The title turns out to refer to the cartoon, *Duck Amok*, an unlikely source that in fact presents a surprisingly accurate model of some of Ashbery's poetry. Where Ginsberg's *Fantasia*-poetics posits the poet as authoritative and singular magician, *Duck Amok* presents the poet as split into two figures: Daffy Duck and Bugs Bunny. The cartoon begins with Daffy striding out dressed as a sailor. But suddenly the background changes from a battleship to Waikiki, while Daffy, now wearing grass skirt and lei, is still swabbing what used to be the deck but is now a beach. He registers this, then begins to dance the hula and strum his ukelele. The backdrop changes to Alaska. After an angry double take, Daffy begins to ski. The changes continue: Daffy is turned into a flower, a cube, he disappears into a black hole, always blowing his top appropriately. Finally the perspective lifts up, revealing that Daffy is on a transparency; up above sits the cartoonist, Bugs, who ends the cartoon by smirking, "Ain't I a stinker?" This explains the preceding visual hijinx, which otherwise would be quite avant-garde for a commercial cartoon. A similar tranquilizing effect occurs at the end of Ashbery's poem except that instead of Bugs, the final figure is a normalizing "we." But the bulk of poem is decidedly untranquil in a way that can be usefully gauged by keeping the Bugs-Daffy duo in mind.

This pair makes for a more conflicted model of expression than the clarity of the poet speaking and creating the truth. Here there is no dichotomy between true and false, only a desire to transgress the registrations of clarity. The goal for the constructor of the statement (Bugs) is to make the constructed statement (Daffy) as glaring as possible in hula skirts and eskimo outfits. Even though most readers would not know the cartoon, an exuberant inappropriateness of language is clearly the poem's motor of desire.

Poetry and sexuality here are not, as for Ginsberg, in the service of clarity. The "I" is compromised from the start: the poem begins, "Something strange is creeping across me." This "something" is, in fact, "everything":

> La Celestina has only to warble the first few bars
> Of "I Thought about You" or something mellow from
> *Amadigi di Gaula* for everything—a mint-condition can
> Of Rumford's Baking Powder, a celluloid earring, Speedy
> Gonazles, the latest from Helen Topping Miller's fertile
> Escritoire, a sheaf of suggestive pix on griege, deckle-edged
> Stock—to come clattering through the rainbow trellis
> Where Pistachio Avenue rams the 2300 block of Highland
> Fling Terrace. (31)

There is nothing natural among this comically reduced yet deeply eccentric "everything." We are not in Ginsberg's Kansas anymore, either; this is the landscape of media—cartoons, fiction, elegant porn—where even the earrings are celluloid. The can of baking powder is only manufactured object, and it's an antique, as if in some aficionado's collection.

Repeated references to sex appear in the midst of camp, virtuoso displays of wrong notes. Readers expecting anything like normal word-to-word sequences—the way Daffy keeps hoping Hawaii will stay Hawaii—will continually be confronted by micro-implausibilities like "a shower of pecky acajou harpoons." Straight characters such as those cartoon bastions of Americana, Walt Skeezix and family, are brought together with the polymorphous Princesse de Clèves to engage in "micturition sprees" and "algolagnic *nuits blanches*." In this context, inappropriateness itself becomes sexualized. Ashbery is displaying a garish sexuality (drawing it on Daffy, so to speak) but not embodying it. Rather than the timeless and dignified pathos of self contemplating its representations that was enacted in "Self-Portrait in a Convex Mirror," we get the following:

> He promised he'd get me out of this one,
> That mean old cartoonist, but just look what he's
> Done to me now! I scarce dare approach me mug's attenuated
> Reflection in yon hubcap, so jaundiced, so *dèconfit*
> are its lineaments (31)

The classic poetic trope on death, "the region from which no traveller returns," becomes

> Wait!
> I have an announcement! This wide, tepidly meandering,
> Civilized Lethe (one can barely make out the maypoles
> And *chaléts de nécessité* on its sedgy shore) leads to Tophet, that
> Landfill-haunted, not-so-residential resort from which
> Some travellers return! (32)

Paradise Lost, naturally enough, is quoted too. Bugs Bunny is thus God and Daffy the metamorphic Satan:

> While I
> Abroad through all the coasts of dark destruction seek
> Deliverance for us all, think in that language: its
> Grammar, though tortured, offers pavilions
> At each new parting of the ways. Pastel
> Ambulances scoop up the quick and hie them to hospitals. (33)

It is dangerous, with Ashbery, to read too much into any particular image, but here, the hospital and ambulances are characteristic in their avoidance of the finality of damnation, which the lines from Milton evoke: the Ashberian traveler can return from death as easily as a cartoon figure can be reconstituted. One can read such avoidances—a constitutive feature of Ashbery's writing— as a force for liberation, where a decentered subject allows for release of the energy normally bound into the signifier. Ashbery's lines create complex hermeneutic perspectives, whereas when Ginsberg writes "Bomb China's 200,000,000 / cried Stennis from Mississippi / I guess it was 3 weeks ago" he is confronting the reader with an insistently stark meaning. Thus Andrew Ross can write that, despite Ashbery's refusal to sign a petition opposing the Vietnam War, Ashbery is engaged in "the only oppositional activity proper to the poet," which is "to expose and thereby impoverish an established class of looking and writing."[22]

The question of whether a decentered subject can be a political agent and oppose centralized power is of course quite problematic. Empirically, a highly centered subject such as Ginsberg has had more effect. But assuming that the figure of a decentered subject stands as a utopian prefiguration of liberation, the question remains to what extent Ashbery's writing *does* posit such a subject. In "Daffy Duck in Hollywood" the style changes radically within and between sentences, there are a number of seemingly different examples of "I," and there is a constant breaking up into new contexts. But as often happens with Ashbery's work after *The Tennis Court Oath*, the games die down at the end. Here, an external landscape begins to peep through, at first in a deliberately outmoded epic simile: "As when / Low skyscrapers from lower-hanging clouds reveal / A turret there, an art-deco escarpment here." There are still some remnants of the subversive combining of sex and Norman Rockwell-esque Americana—"Grab sex things, swing up / Over the horizon like a boy / On a fishing expedition"—but in the overall motion of the poem "we" are finally placed in the outer world. The precondition is that politics, domestic or international, be pushed away:

> This mulch for
> Play keeps them interested and busy while the big,
> Vaguer stuff can decide what it wants—what maps, what
> Model cities, how much waste space. Life, our
> Life, anyway, is between. We don't mind
> Or notice any more that the sky *is* green, a parrot
> One, (34)

Here the pressures of the historical context become visible: Johnson's Model Cities program and maps of Vietnam are the concern of "the big, / Vaguer stuff" (note the coincidence with "vaguely realizing westward"). These excisions mean "we" live "in between." While some of the prior cartoon extravagance continues to infect or enliven this locale in the form of a parrot-green sky, our life is finally normal, even though it's in a reduced world. We

> have our earnest where it chances on us,
> Disingenuous, intrigued, inviting more,
> Always invoking the echo, a summer's day.

For Ashbery, such summer days, with their disingenuous allegiance to the empirical world, are a home for a particularly rich variety of poetry. For many language writers, they are not.

Anti-Map: Barrett Watten's *Progress*

I will begin my brief survey of self and mapping in language writing with
Barrett Watten's *Progress*, a book-length poem written in the early eighties.
Where Frost could call the roll sonorously, "She was ours / In Massachusetts,
in Virginia," Watten makes a disidentification with his physical and political
surroundings one of the foundations of his poetry:

> The poetry is this distance
>   Given in place of names.
>   Idaho, Vermont, Louisiana
> Fall out of sky,
>   onto plains . . . .[23]

Rather than an emotional, representative figure who presents the identifying
reader with the naturalized arena of "the land," we have an assertion of "distance." When quoted alone, the ellipses here might seem expressive of a voice
trailing off, but they are in fact a uniform feature of the poem, ending each
five-line stanza and furnishing a flexible hinge to the next. Vermont, Idaho,
and Louisiana form a strikingly separated trio, both geographically and historically. The fact that they "fall out of sky" enhances their arbitrariness; they are
not locales for personal experience. The next stanza confirms this:

>   Idaho, Vermont, Louisiana
> Fall out of sky,
>   onto plains . . . .
>
> But only a plane of discourse. (48)

The tone can seem impersonal, almost bureaucratic, especially if measured
against the linguistic resources Ginsberg and Ashbery use in their oppositional
moments. Compare the forces "Daffy Duck" deploys against its target: "The
bizarrely but effectively equipped infantries of happy-go-nutty / Vegetal jac-
queries, plumed, pointed at the little / White cardboard castle over the mill
run" (32); or Ginsberg enlisting Blake, Whitman, and a panoply of divinities
against the war: "I call all Powers of imagination / . . . / Shambu Bharti Baba
naked covered with ash / Khaki Baba fat-bellied mad with the dogs / . . . /
Sacred Heart my Christ acceptable / Allah the Compassionate One / Jaweh
Righteous One / . . . . / Let the States tremble, / let the Nation weep" (126–
28). In contrast with Ginsberg's prophetic self or Ashbery's fantastical self-
division, Watten seems intent on disavowing any investment in the self:

> It all comes back in words
>> Measured against a movement
> Of shipping in channels. . . .
>
> In the Panama Canal.
>> Specify
> *I* to know what this means, (64)

Impersonality is built into the poem: proper names occur at flexibly programmed intervals; the pronoun "I" appears once within the space of every six stanzas. It is at times italicized, used as a noun in analytic phrases ("The pronoun *I* as a business / Letter," [74]; "scan / Of *I* breaks down to habits," [93]), or placed after its verb for further alienation ("*Excite I* a map of my position," 120). In this dispersed environment, the proper names—Mussolini, Miami, Watts, Union City—seem intensely singular, emblematic of a gnomic totality.

But to describe *Progress* as systematically impersonal discourse is to miss the charged spirit of contradiction that animates the writing, making statements such as "The poetry is this distance" difficult to fathom. If we continue the passage quoted above, the dynamics of the poem's negativity will become clearer:

> But only a plane of discourse.
>> I give blessing to this
>> Paucity of means,
>>> it is not
> An explanation made gratuitous. . . .
>
> But life and death itself.
>> Only 45 minutes by timer
>> To interrupt primary myth.
> Note hatred of content,
>> face. . . . (48–49)

In my reading, the "I" here is a standard marker of self and the "plane of discourse" is not a preordained poststructuralist fact but a condition that has been achieved by an ascetic act of renunciation—"I give blessing to this / Paucity of means." Taking leave of the physical plains which Frost claimed and which so troubled Ginsberg as he drove through them is both a matter of utmost importance for Watten, and something mechanical: both "life and death" and a process involving "45 minutes by timer" (possibly the time of one writing session). "Note hatred of content": an "I" is missing from this clipped statement, but not the author's emotion. The content—of the world? of the poem?—is not simply held at an impersonal distance, it is loathed.

One factor contributing to this hatred is that the act of distancing is only partially successful. Almost any passage will show self and external social materials engaged in a rapid, contradictory confrontation. Rather than a dispersed "I" yielding unobstructed access to an unproblematic plane of discourse, the real-time self often reemerges, uncomfortably, into a material history that has precious little space for it:

> An intermediary in a likeness
> > Of a bureaucrat in a frame
> > On wall of doctor's office,
> Humphrey,
> > > meanwhile the war. . . .
>
> One believes has been overcome
> > To write about it,
> > > surfaces
> > As a complex sport in which
> Men try to keep their balance. . . .
>
> On floating logs,
> > > later to be
> > Knocked off by competitors
> > Into the swirling detritus
> And sucked down into a hole. . . .
>
> Reappearing on the other side
> > Of a public works project
> > Reborn in a line of men
> Waiting,
> > > and I am one of them. . . . (96)

The agents of the Vietnam War at the beginning of this passage are not, as in "Wichita Vortex Sutra," demonic magicians to be bested by counter-spells, but cogs of large bureaucratic structures, "intermediaries," "bureaucrats in a frame"—governors or CEOs whose photographs adorn the offices of underlings. This awareness leads "one" to believe the war can be written about and will fit into the poem. ("One" is a more accurate indicator of Watten's position in *Progress* than "I": it is not subject to rhetorical displacement.) But the scale of history makes any individual statement slippery, as the image in subsequent stanzas dramatizes. "One," the self, becomes one of many: soldiers, athletes, workers—disposable units in any case. And they are disposed of after their pessimistic balancing acts: "sucked down into a hole." This does not necessarily represent anything like death; in fact it seems more like business as usual, as the men, losers in capital's log-rolling contests, rematerialize to stand in line idly near a public-works project, the kind of site dismissed at the end of "Daffy Duck."

In a discussion of *Progress* Watten says that "political figures enter into the poem as lexical items in a dissociative discourse."[24] But the war does not fit easily into the poem. His rationale changes considerably when it comes to the following lines: "McNamara, / Johnson, Westmoreland, Rusk. / The names are no pun intended" (111). Concerning these figures, Watten says, "when I got to end of the poem I was just writing what I had to say. . . . I always wanted a poem that would . . . intend a meaning for those names." The war made this desire urgent: "read[ing] the accounts of Hanoi being bombed . . . every day . . . was like another wound. And McNamara, Johnson, Westmoreland, Rusk, and Nixon, who appears later, Kissinger also, were the agents of this situation that I wished with my entire being to deny." This negativity "became a form of the self." Watten meant, via the act of writing, to undo the power that they had over him: "to put them into the poem is to trade the agency they had as initiators . . . for whatever the text now is. . . . [I]t's to put them on paper and have them to some extent objectified, and thereby transformed. . . . I'm arguing for a different use of them, not a fantastic recuperation of wounds but a direct naming and almost an adjudication of them, which dispenses with them. It's only in the logic of the poem, in this form, that I feel the proper distance can be taken from McNamara, Johnson, Westmoreland, Rusk" (46–48).

If we turn to the passage in question, the distance will be undeniable. But whether it is the proper distance for historical judgment is another matter:

> McNamara,
> Johnson, Westmoreland, Rusk.
> The names are no pun intended. . . .
>
> A present dispensing its edges,
> But I call them Bald Eagles
> For lust,
> lusty and silly
> Happy and holy men and girls. . . .

> An irritation,
>> etymology beats
>> Its curse into the ground. (111–12)

"No pun intended" suggests, to my ear at least, that a very obvious pun has been made. But rather than a pun, the list seems to be an ethical tautology: if these men are malignant, then here is malignancy personified. The "adjudication" that Watten claims for these lines in the interview seems to have been swallowed up by the bare act of naming, and it remains quite private. Rather than objectified and distanced, the names seem closely bound up with the author.[25] The subsequent stanzas bear this out to an extent, veering between sardonic irony ("lusty and silly / Happy and holy men and girls"), understatement ("An irritation"), and a curse.[26]

In the interview I have been citing, Watten draws a contrast between himself and Ginsberg at various points. Ginsberg, he says, embodies the "erotic other of normative social discourse" (39) and, by the extremity of his self-revelation, invites the reader to identify with him. Watten characterizes his own practice as evoking "a sort of anti-identification, an anti-response" (51). In a large sense, this is quite true: the distance by which *Progress* attempts to master the political field is very different from Ginsberg's engaged naming. But as I have indicated, this distance is far from secure. There are repeated quick breaks in the willed abstraction of the language: when Watten blesses his access to the plane of discourse or curses the ground that fails to conform to it, he is, like Ginsberg, invoking the dimension of the sacred.[27]

Such invocation seems far from the characteristic gesture of *Progress*, which involves the forceful, highly oppositional positing of conditions. "The poetry *is* this distance, / *Given* in place of names" (my italics); or the opening of the poem:

> Relax,
>> stand at attention, and.
>> Purple snake stands out on
>> Porcelain tiles. The idea
> *Is* the thing. *Skewed* by design. . . . (1) [second italics mine]

Who is doing the giving and the skewing? Whose distance and whose design is this? While the grammar is impersonal, I hear in these copulas and participles a great desire for power, which is understandable if one is trying to intervene in the political landscape. In an interview, Watten comments that the ubiquity of the American flag unites ideology and psychology, resulting in "an auratic excess of national glory." He, on the other hand, is interested in "an

American flag in its complementary colors, [green, black, and orange], that, given its ubiquitous repetition, would have the opposite effect. Some of the statements in my poems I hope might work that way when experienced cumulatively."[28] This seems an apt summary of his poetic-political intentions. But the difference in scale between poet and government will mean that all the communiques issued by the poet will be charged with tremendous frustration: the green, black, and orange antiflags will remain negative subsets of Old Glory. One can assert that the idea *is* the thing, but despite the italic emphasis, the things remain.

Gendered Maps

I will now look at the configurations of self and space in the work of Beverly Dahlen, Susan Howe, Rae Armantrout, and Carla Harryman. The work of these women, while quite different from one another, will not display the same automatic access (whether positive or negative) to larger political and cultural mappings that we have seen in Frost, Ginsberg, Ashbery, and Watten. Alternate routes to power are under construction. But while I think that gender is often implicated in writers' maps, I distrust categories that obliterate the complexities of the writing: statements combining sociology and poetry are particularly vexed. There is no essential woman language writer that these four exemplify, nor does Barrett Watten represent the male language writer. And in fact it would be more accurate to describe Dahlen and Howe not as language writers but as "associated with language writing." Howe began her career as a painter and her writing developed in relative isolation; Dahlen's work was already in process when the initial interactions of language writing began in the seventies: she is closely associated with the group that coalesced around the journal *HOW(ever)* founded by Kathleen Fraser.[29] Nevertheless, despite the anti-exemplariness of these writers—Armantrout and Harryman are not 'typical' of language writing either—gender will be a crucial influence on their mapping.

Dahlen has described her ongoing project, *A Reading*, as "something like a journal, at times like poetry, or prose narrative. . . . Its method . . . aspires to be free association."[30] But she immediately qualifies "free" by juxtaposing Lacan's comment that free association is more like "forced labor," that "nothing could be less free."[31] Elsewhere she writes, "Freud said self-analysis is impossible, and I agree."[32] This is the site of *A Reading*: a knot of free (slave) association and self-scrutiny that might also be self-censorship.

A Reading begins: "before that and before that. everything in a line" (15).[33] These two sentences contain, in embryonic form, an opposition that will be repeated throughout. The writing moves in a contradictory direction to what might ultimately be its meaning. The possible content that the writing tries to read is pushed backward to some unreachable Eden (left of the left margin); while the writing itself, moving to the right, defers, masks, betrays the presence that it cannot represent.

The more the writing tries to objectify its content, or perhaps to call a content into existence, the less present any content becomes:

> blank, it was a rule of thumb, black thumb, someone's new press, imprint, printer's ink. how could you call that a clock? it was winding, trailing, the shadows filling up the forest on a June evening, I was reading that, reading it with a falling for summer which is always long ago and far away. even in childhood it never came, it was a fairy tale, something to look back on. I cannot tell myself a straightforward story. (32)

If presence in language is always incomplete, what is to stop the restless back and forth of attempted naming? It is easily conceivable that almost any passage could keep on going. Formally, *A Reading* is a sustained wrestling with the problem of what its form could possibly be. But this is not solely due to the inaccessibility of the unconscious:

> all those women. how they tried to be a conscience for one another. how lying seemed their native tongue.

> not to say William, bilious, not to echo, repeat what won't come clear, not to be caught here in sticking in the throat. gagging. the saying not to say. we covered it up but were found out anyway. it was done in the open. that's where the wind comes, for wind read calm, and the darkness, and for darkness read light. that's where she is one or another so must be both. the murdered or murderer.

> think of it. choosing chooses all. drags in the cat's tail Arcturus far star clouds of glory. this is talk. talk is cheap.

> the interminable reading. the infinite analysis. (17)

This last paragraph refers to Freud's "Analysis Terminable and Interminable." If the title is construed as a question, "terminable" should, according to Freud, be the correct answer: men should be realistic about masculinity (i.e., they should accept the passivity toward other men that social hierarchy inevitably brings) and women should be realistic about masculinity (i.e., they should give up all desire for it). But here, when therapy should be over, interminability seems most firmly entrenched: "At no point in one's analytic work does one suffer more from the oppressive feeling . . . that one is 'talking to the winds' than when one is trying to persuade a female patient to abandon her wish for a penis on the ground of its being unreasonable, or to convince a male patient that a passive attitude towards another man does not always signify castration."[34]

Freud finds the perpetual intrusion of gender unreasonable; Dahlen finds it perpetually stuck in her throat. She continually asserts the fact of and the impossibility of being a woman and writing out of that situation. Women, having only the patriarchal language to speak, must either choke ("sticking in the throat. gagging. the saying not to say") or lie ("how lying seemed their native tongue"). In this context the allusion to "Intimations of Immortality" ("drags in the cat's tail Arcturus far star clouds of glory") seems particularly bitter. For Wordsworth the child born "trailing clouds of glory" is, of course, male; at six he is "Fretted by sallies of his mother's kisses / With light upon him from his father's eyes," and the light-filled paradise that birth echoes is always available to the somberer (male) adult in possession of "the philosophic mind"—Dahlen might term it, "the phallocratic mind." Her vision of birth and what it bequeaths the writer is much harsher:

> she who is absolutely other coming out of the dark. myself as the dark. in the dark. watching in silence the shadows. alone. . . . "Who's in charge here?" Grace asks in Kathleen's poem. is anyone in charge? what would I do about it, baby or no baby, finally I did not have to make that decision. made in the dark. the blood. blood. garbage. it is all garbage, I told him. all this. reading the waste, the excrement. the entrails of animals. what's left in the cup. after the tea is gone, after the party's over. (76–77)

There is none of Wordsworth's hoped-for celestial patrimony here; the difficulties produced by birth (or by being born female) preclude any cosmic harmony. A woman is "absolutely other"; she is confronted with a real choice about having a child or not; birth is a bloody mess. Rather than the site of reconciliation with nature, language marks the birth of permanent alienation. The mother, for Dahlen, does more than fret the child with sallies of kisses. Near the end of Part Five, the following quote from Kristeva's *Desire in Language* is interspersed in the text: "the *entry in syntax constitutes a first victory over the mother*. . . . suggests that naming, always originating in a place (the *chora*, space, "topic," subject-predicate) is a *replacement* for what the speaker perceives as an archaic mother—a more or less victorious confrontation, never finished with her."[35]

This archaic space is what Dahlen wants to map. But the features of this mapping (words) are all phallic, in the Lacanian sense, which leaves the reality Dahlen is trying to read out of reach:

Phallus the first division, woman atomized . . . what is real in this fantasy of the real is the phallus. everybody believes it. I believe it. you can't touch it with a ten foot pole because it isn't there. that's how it comes to be real. it isn't there. and I'm not here. nobody's here and that's reality. (85)

However, there is one knowable fact in *A Reading*: the impossibility resulting from gender:

that X which was laid over it ages ago. no wonder I am a woman. now. impossible. woman, that impossibility. (78)

Dahlen is at her most authoritative in the midst of such assertions of impossibility:

anything may mean its opposite, green may mean red, you can't tell an omen when you see one. reading it. must we go on reading as if we lived in the sixteenth century.

(All this language is floating. The men make statements. They use the forms of the verb 'to be' with confidence. What I write is provisional. It depends. It is subject to constant modification. It depends.)

(Equivalence.)

(They are so sure this equals that. Reading their sums.)

on the other hand. all dark. blank. the blank wall waiting. in it. waiting for something, The Other. (76)

The capitals beginning sentences—occurring only here—may be taken phallic-parodically, with Dahlen stylistically masquerading as male; nevertheless, it is difficult to take anything in this passage as its opposite. The assertion of provisionality is convincing as assertion, not as provisionality. At such times it becomes difficult to tell the tentativeness of Dahlen's quasi-identity as a woman writing apart from the assurance that a male writer is said to feel.

A Reading is systematic in its perpetual assertion of gender-negativity; in this antigenerality it resembles *Progress.* Susan Howe's work, on the other hand, explores space in a mode of extreme particularity: in some works this is thematized as a desperate wandering through a dangerous wilderness, with particular historical figures such as Mary Rowlandson and Hope Atherton offered as models for a writer and a reader who are only given the most contingent glimpse of where they are.[36] Often her page bears a resemblance to a chart of an archaeological dig. But there is no systematic apprehension; she is trying to place pieces of processes that have left only fragments. Consider the prose note that begins "Thorow." Howe describes a lonely stint teaching a poetry workshop in Lake George, New York:

> During the winter and spring of 1987. . . . I rented a cabin . . . at the edge of the lake. The town, or what is left of a town, is a travesty. Scores of two-star motels have been arbitrarily scrambled between gas stations and gift shops selling Indian trinkets, china jugs shaped like breasts with nipples for spouts, American flags in all shapes and sizes, and pornographic bumper-stickers. . . . a fake fort where a real one once stood, a Dairy-Mart, a Donut-land, and a four-star Ramada Inn built over an ancient Indian burial ground. Everything graft, everything grafted. . . . After I learned to keep out of town, and after the first panic of dislocation had subsided, I moved into the weather's fluctuation. . . .
>
> **Narrative in Non-Narrative**
>
> . . . Lake George was a blade of ice to write across not knowing what She.
> Interior assembling of forces underneath earth's eye. Yes, she, the Strange, excluded from formalism. I heard poems inhabited by voices.
> In the seventeenth century European adventurer-traders burst through the forest to discover this particular long clear body of fresh water. They brought our story to it. Pathfinding believers in God and grammar spelled the lake into *place*. They have renamed it several times since. In paternal colonial systems a positivist efficiency appropriates primal indeterminacy.
> In March, 1987, looking for what is looking, I went down to unknown regions of indifferentiation. The Adirondacks *occupied* me.[37]

The accuracy of the opening survey of trinkets and fakery makes a welcome supplement to Frostian encomiums to "the land." The juxtaposition of flags and dirty bumper stickers is one aspect of the critique, but the china breasts for dispensing milk are even more telling. America may still be bountiful, but beneath the haze of sentiment over the landscape, "she" is a highly adminis-tered and commodified cornucopia.

The primary difference between the two kinds of mapping here is both obvious and provocative. The gap between "she, the Strange" and the china breasts is a large one. But the two halves of this passage are not that easy to separate fully; to label one "narrative" and the other "nonnarrative" would be to ignore the fact that quite a bit of the second half is involved with narrative. Some elements there could be construed as Frostian or even "Sharp-

Implement." "Moving into the weather's fluctuation," could be a possible line in a poem committed to historical vagueness. And the end of the passage, "The Adirondacks *occupied* me," is similar, except for the pronoun, to Frost's trope: "Possessing what we still were unpossessed by." But there are major differences. There are no Donut-lands in "The Gift Outright." The historicizing vision that sees "Pathfinding believers in God and grammar spell[ing] the lake into *place*" is not to be found in Frost: the critique that links a patriarchal God and grammar would be anathema to Frost's commitment to "iambic lines and colloquial speech patterns." "They have renamed it several times since" is a deadpan noticing that a would-be transcendent act is in reality quite contingent: it is exactly what Frost's reliance on Massachusetts as a "lying European word" wants to mask.

Recall the odd phrasing in the anthology note near the beginning of the chapter: Frost positioned himself against "nothingness and the free verse experiments" of the modernists. Even though Howe's invocation of "She" contains a slight resemblance to the feminized land of "The Gift Outright," there is a tremendous difference here, both in Howe's willingness to confront the possible "nothingness" of the landscape and in her reliance of modernist linguistic dislocations: "Lake George was a blade of ice to write across not knowing what She."

These dislocations, which are often reflected by the spacing on the page, make up the bulk of her writing. Peter Quartermain discusses Howe's linguistic, typographic irregularities and their relation to the normative empire of meaning: the voices that history has made anonymous "have been hidden by a utilitarian, canonizing, and classisizing impulse . . . which, patriarchal, seeks to possess the text by removing or rationalizing all 'accidentals,' confining it to a single body of meaning."[38] This seems quite accurate, save that the "patriarchal" impulse is not simply an external enemy in Howe's work. The "European adventurer-traders . . . brought *our* story" to Lake George (my italics). Her writing is on both sides.

Thus in "A Bibliography of the King's Book or, Eikon Basilike," the following passage will be thematically crucial. The "King's Book," supposedly authored by King Charles just before his beheading, was according to Milton, a fake: one of its prayers paraphrased a love poem from Sidney's *Arcadia*, which Howe describes as "the prayer of a pagan woman to an all-seeing heathen Deity." She goes on to comment: "A captive Shepherdess has entered through a gap in ideology."[39] But while this outlines one of Howe's principal concerns, most of the piece inhabits the territory of Milton's condemnation, even while critiquing it. Howe never pretends that she can fully *hear* the suppressed voices.

In "Thorow" there is no separating the antinomian wilderness from the activities of the occupying settlers. Howe takes up an ambiguous middle position, as a "scout": "Author the real author / acting the part of a scout" (51). The writing explores the margins of civilization and wilderness without specifying which side the words are on:

Mortal particulars
whose shatter we are

A sort of border life
A single group of trees

. . . .

Young pine in a stand of oak
young oak in a stand of pine (50)

Thoreau is quoted as praising the original crookedness of the land and language: "am glad to see that you have studied out the ponds, got the Indian names straightened out—which means made more crooked"; but in the next paragraph his own is made crooked, as Howe cites *A New Passage to Cataia*, which was written "To proove that the Indians aforenamed came not by the Northeast, and that there is no thorow passage navigable that way" (42). The title of the piece, "Thorow," acknowledges this condition of being stuck in a place that has no transcendent entrance or exit.

In the following passage, Indian names are made "crooked" by some settler's imperfect orthography, but would Thoreau have approved?

at Fort Stanwix the Charrokey
paice

only from that Alarm
all those Guards

Constant parties of guards
up & down

Agreseror

Bearer law my fathers

Revealing traces
Regulating traces (46)

Names are misspelled on both sides of the European/Indian divide. The last couplet asserts that there is no revelation of traces without regulation of them. Intelligibility cannot meet the unknown without rendering it—but only partially—intelligible.

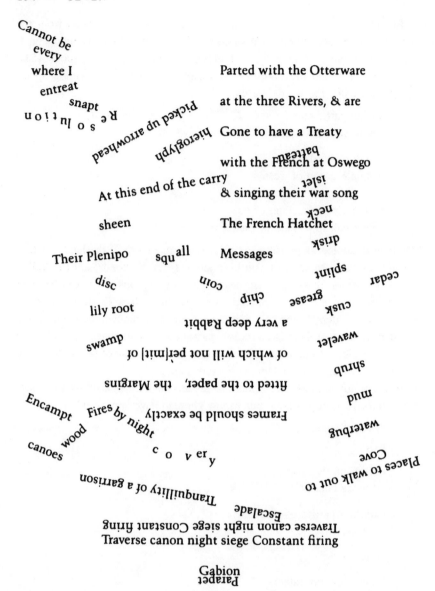

Cannot be
every
where I   Parted with the Otterware
entreat
snapt   at the three Rivers, & are
Re s o lu t i o n
picked up arrowhead   hieroglyph Gone to have a Treaty
battered
with the French at Oswego
At this end of the carry   islet
& singing their war song
neck
sheen   The French Hatchet
dink
Their Plenipo   squall   Messages
splint   cedar
disc   coin
chip   grease
lily root
a very deep Rabbit   cusk
wavelet
swamp
of which will not per[mit] of
shrub
fitted to the paper,   the Margins
mud
Encampt Fires by night   Frames should be exactly
waterbug
wood
canoes   c o v er y   Cove
places to walk out to
Tranquillity of a garrison
Escalade
Traverse canon night siege Constant firing
Traverse canon night siege Constant firing

Gabion
Parapet

Figure 4. (56)

The two-page spread reproduced here (Figures 4 and 5 [56,57]) displays this reciprocal incommensurability. Various patches of text more or less mirror one another across the divide. Signs of European military strength and civilization are right side up on the right-hand page: "Parapets"; "Tranquillity of a garrison"; instructions for accurate bookmaking: "The Frames should be

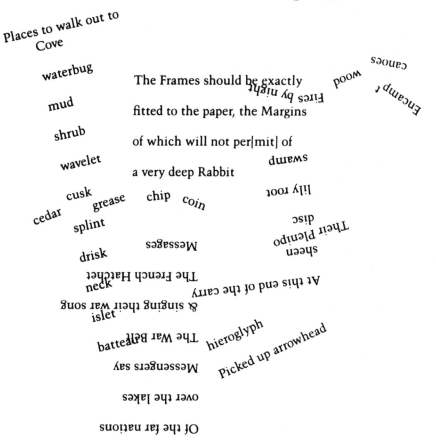

Figure 5. (57)

exactly / fitted to the paper, the Margins / of which will not per[mit] of / a very deep Rabbit." Across on the facing page these are upside down, with phrases that seem to come from scouts placed, more or less, right side up: "Encampt," "Fires by night," et cetera. While there is a general binary structure loosely in place here, it is contradicted in many "local" patches of these pages.

I'll close my discussion by mentioning two small snarls. First, the small couplet "hieroglyph / Picked up arrowhead," which very economically mixes hostility and semi-intelligibility without resolving them. And second, an even smaller pair: "disc," halfway down the left side of Figure 4, and "covery," disposed shakily near the bottom slightly left of center. While much of Howe's writing works toward discovery of semi-erased traces of suppressed lives, she seems aware that her own investigation can never escape the possibility that she is simply adding another layer over what it wants to reveal: "discovery" may always be "covery." This is the dilemma that the warring singularities of her work reveal.

Rae Armantrout's poems rely tenaciously on the intelligibility of language, though the world is finally no more lucid for all that. A few particulars of the San Diego landscape, where the poet lives, are focused on very clearly; however, just outside the field of focus is a strong penumbra of unease: gender has everything to do with this. I will read two of her recent poems. First, "The Garden":

> Oleander: coral
> from lipstick ads in the 50's.
>
> Fruit of the tree of *such* knowledge.
>
> To "smack"
> (thin air)
> meaning kiss or hit.
>
> It appears
> in the guise of outworn usages
> because we are bad?
>
> Big masculine threat,
> insinuating and slangy.[40]

Such compressed, yet far-reaching work needs detailed unpacking. Line 1 begins simply, with two named, natural things. The colon between them should be a sign of junction or equality, yet the equation opens up a paradox: oleander doesn't equal coral. Named, natural things seem to have been yoked into artificial human schemes. One can normalize this by saying that the poet has seen some oleander and realized that it's the same color she remembers from old lipstick ads. True enough, perhaps, but the bare typography can work the other way: rather than suggesting a consolidating moment of memory, it would indicate an alienating moment of insight into the fact that artificial nature imagery has replaced nature and become an arsenal of images for painting women into a "natural" corner. Named and natural will turn out to be antithetic in Armantrout's work.

However real "*such* knowledge" may be, knowledge not of nature but of fashion systems, it is the fruit that is available to the poet. Mentioning the tree of knowledge extends the poem's discord back to the title. Rather than a pleasant garden-vignette, "The Garden" now refers to the original garden, where woman brought sin into the world. In the next stanza she gets smacked for it. But perhaps the woman is just being paranoid: isn't she being kissed, admired in her coral lipstick? The stanza equivocates—"kiss or hit"—which ultimately has the effect of equating violence and the standard protocols of male affection toward women.

The next stanza brings up "outworn usages": perhaps all this is dated, just like the old lipstick ads. But the question of whether this is because "we are bad" throws us back well before the fifties, back to the Garden of Eden again. "It" at the beginning of the stanza seems to refer to this tautological cycle of guilt: does woman's deficiency need to be covered up by alienated bits of nature—old coral lipstick—because she is deficient?

The final stanza turns this guilt outward. The system of nature now in place, the Garden, is finally perceived not to be feminine—woman as flower—but to function as a "Big masculine threat." However, things are not so cut and dried; the poet is not safe because she has identified the threat. The masculine system of sin and nature remains "insinuating": it is very much in her language. This insinuation is temporal as well: the Garden was not just a problem back in fifties, an obstacle for Mom's generation, it is in the present of language as well, even its future, if slang is seen as anticipating the future of speech.

"The Garden" gives us only one small particular—an oleander—before the sea of gender trouble washes over it. In "Necromance,"[41] more of the present is visible. It is a somewhat longer poem, and so I will comment between stanzas:

> Poppy under a young
> pepper tree, she thinks.
> The Siren always sings
> like this. Morbid
> glamor of the singular.
> Emphasizing correct names
> as if making amends.

The first line and a half could be read as factual. But as in "The Garden," punctuation and gender quickly interrupt the smooth plane of realism. The comma in line 2 can be read in a stronger sense than as simply marking a verb of thinking. There is the outer world and, comma, here she is, separated, thinking. In line 3 she is a Siren, or hears the Siren inside her, singing her thought. Sirens are illicit, highlighting the narcotic quality of the first word, "Poppy," which now seems closer to one of Circe's drugs than to contemporary realism. In fact, the clarity of single, named things is a narcotic siren song: "Morbid / glamor of the singular." It is doubtful that the poet is hearing this song at a manfully repressed distance like Odysseus; more likely she is close to the siren: poets are supposed to sing after all. By the fourth sentence the relation of language and things has become the opposite of the neutral descriptive beginning. Accuracy has become a kind of expiation, though it is not clear who feels it necessary to make amends to whom.

> Ideal
> republic of the separate
> dust motes
> afloat in abeyance.
> Here the sullen
> come to see their grudge
> as pose, modelling.

> The flame trees tip themselves
> with flame.
> But in that land
> men prized
> virginity. She washed
> dishes in a black liquid
> with islands of froth—
> and sang.

The second stanza begins with a sarcastic political credo. We might avoid the morbidity of glamor if we did away with gender and in fact with life, if people were dust motes. Like many of Armantrout's connections, this is heavily metaphorical. In the third stanza, she turns on this impulse, suggesting that what underlies realistic description is gendered metaphorics. In a 'real,' i.e., masculine world, what else could the flame trees tip themselves but flame? This may seem thoroughly obvious; however, the next sentence, beginning with "But," seems to find a problem with it. Putting these two sentence together leads to the conclusion that such naming is a sexual act. Accurate naming, like an overly predictable marriage, can seem a tautology, leading men to desire fresh conquests. This situation, where men always want to be Adam, naming and possessing the glamorous, singular woman for the first time, leaves the poet-Siren stuck at the sink. But she sings witchily, creating deceptive islands in a sea of death: more morbid glamor of the singular.

> Couples lounge
> in slim, fenced yards
> beside the roar
> of a freeway. Huge pine
> a quarter-mile off
> floats. Hard to say where
> this occurs.

Here we are back in the real world of real marriages. However, given the strong links between realism and masculinity that have been showing up, it is not surprising that this return to the real would be guarded by a gigantic phallic pine. "Hard to say where / this occurs" recalls Dahlen's Lacanian outcry: "what is real in this fantasy of the real is the phallus. everybody believes it. I believe it. you can't touch it with a ten foot pole because it isn't there."

> Third dingy
> bird-of-paradise
> from right. Emphatic
> precision
> is revealed as
> hostility. It is
> just a bit further.
>
> The mermaid's
> privacy.

But the poet gives us directions on how to get to that impossible place, "here": "Third dingy / bird-of-paradise / from right." If one hears the biblical echo in "bird-of-paradise," Armantrout, as in "The Garden," is connecting the specific (and tacky) San Diego cityscape with the gender wars that emanate from the Garden of Eden. The contemporary landscape and the contemporary language may be precise, but they contain hostile distances, within which women remain private, mythological creatures.

Isolated images, often paired down close to single words, are the sites of such sexual, social conflicts. In "Context" this is made particularly clear. Armantrout contrasts "clustered / berries" with "desultory or / 'lonely' // puddles, drops." These in turn are juxtaposed with "Circles an old woman's / fingers trace / on the nubs of / her chair arms." Such minimalism is fraught with the pleasures and dangers of gendered existence:

> Waits for the word to come
> to her, tensed
> as if for orgasm.
>
> Fear surrounds language.[42]

The last work I will discuss will be Carla Harryman's *In the Mode Of*. Questions of pleasure and fear will be encoded in single words here as well, but Harryman's use of mixed modes—narrative, play, stretches of didactic essay—allows her to explore her material from numerous angles; in the final section she attempts to narrate a condition beyond gender. It's a provocative story. *In the Mode Of* is ambitious and highly playful, and its four sections differ greatly from one another; my reading will be selective.

I'll begin by presenting her investigation of two words, "of" and "if." Far from abstract, "of" is the patriarchal word *par excellence*. In the midst of a chaotic parody of a TV discussion, the announcer proposes as a topic: "The government of the people." A voice responds: "What is the government of the people? What does it invoke? What narrative? Not only are we supposedly the authors of our country, a dubious assertion, and not only does the country exist for us, depending on who us is who the vested interest is, but it is as if we are genetically tied. The child is of the mother, blood related. The government is of the people, like the child." A second voice carries the critique further: "The government of, is the rounding up of, herding of dumb beasts. . . . Who wants this government?"[43]

Harryman then illustrates the violent confusion of genetic and political re-production via a fairy tale. A little girl in Iraq experiences the Gulf War as the incursion of "the mendacious sycophants," who wield military power as well as such meta-generalizations as "of." The girl—though not her city—is saved through the advice of a cloud, which tells her that she must resist the designa-tions of the mendacious sycophants who will want her to divide good from bad, "the good people from the bad. The good weapons from the bad. The good governments from the bad" (25). She succeeds in this, overcoming temptations along the way, and therefore remains united with her mother. But she does not abandon designation. In fact, in a list that is devised to problema-tize the lesson the little girl learns, she "calls the water water and the sky sky and people people. She calls agriculture and nature agriculture and nature, music music and silence silence, the Kurds, the Palestinians, the Turks, the Jewish, the Muslims, the Christians, the Kurds, the Palestinians, the Turks, the Jewish, the Muslims, the Christians, she calls a cloud a cloud" (27–28). The beginning and the end of this encase the geopolitical turbulence of history in the blandest tautology.

It is one thing to be able to resist moral generalization and to differentiate "Iraq" from "the people *of* Iraq." The critique of "of" seems clear enough: if its force is accepted uncritically, then "one body becomes part of another body. . . . The distinction between one thing and another, one person and another, is leveled and consumed. (The daughter of Bob). . . . A conduit of aggression and destruction. . . . If OF were a mythological character it would be the god of illusion and instability" (30).

But the names of collectivities remain problematic. Are Kurds Kurds the way water is water? And are they good or bad? Abandoning the fairy tale, Harryman reports on a demonstration where she saw a man carrying a placard that read, "I am a Queer Jew against the Israeli Occupation of the Palestinian People." This message, she writes, "proposes a relationship with what's hidden and marginalized, homosexuality, with the diminishment of and aggression upon race. It differentiates people from governments. . . . [It shifts] value from property to the living. [It acknowledges] the body as reality" (31–32).

The final section, starting as essay and ending as narrative, focuses on this reality, but not in a way that enhances stability of category. The problematic question of identity is given an equally problematic gendered twist: "Male and female. Is one thing we generally know about ourselves if only in a block-headed and parsimonious manner. If female then not male. If male then not female" (34). Rather than OF with its claims of lineage, the ruling preposition of this section is IF, which gives access to the possibility of change. In the present, Harryman writes, "female sociality. . . . start[s] in the 'we've been had' position." But "this inexorable consciousness will create its own self-devouring mechanism. . . . We will see each other first as sets of gestures, postures" (34).

Under the liberating sign of IF, Harryman then rehearses this future in an intimate, antirealistic narrative. It is complex and I will comment on only a few moments of it. One of the most telling of these is in fact before the narrative starts:

> If I could identify the usurpers I would. There are no new fitting names or titles. All those in use sound antiquarian. What I am referring to is in limbo between history and novelty. Like a story. But the destroyer of the story, instead. . . . Is there a place for me in the obstructed story? I will conclude now that "I" am no more than the story. The "I" identifies with the story in a neutral light. There is no neutral light; therefore, "I" do not know my own sex. (33)

Having written the narrator into this situation, Harryman then places her/him in front of an Emil Nolde nude. The story becomes quite raunchy, but the excitement it generates is illicit in more ways than one. In the company of a collector, the narrator muses on the represented nude:

> standing in front of an expressionist nude, trying to decide how I would view this nude if I were a man and how I would view this nude if I were a woman. If. One is a woman then it is likely she has studied how men look at nudes. If. One is a man has one studied the way a woman looks at nudes? . . . She is, possibly, grotesque, but also possibly completely voluptuous with just some kind of male agony infused into her, so that you can't really see her except through the pain the artist has associated with her. This is why her knees are pinched together, her ass is jutting toward me though also twisting away and her head is turned to look at me with great suspicion, or it is just turning away as a gesture of repulsion in which she sees in me, which is what I see in myself if I were a man and want to grab her pussy. Which I do want to do. But am I a man? And is it her pussy? Or mine I would grab first? (36)

The combination of a liberated viewer and an image of bondage is provocative, especially since the viewer does not shut herself/himself off from the power of the image. While there is no verbal similarity, there clearly is a thematic one with Adrienne Rich's "Diving Into the Wreck." There, to recall a few of the well-known lines, "the words are maps," but not to the murky new transgendered territory Rich wants to explore. As she dives down into it, she splits, becoming "the mermaid whose dark hair / streams black, the merman in his armored body. / . . . . / I am she: I am he."[44]

The final narrative of *In the Mode of* differs from this in a number of important ways. Rich's poem is a fully realized allegory, with the sunken ship, the water, diving apparatus, all bearing clearly defined meanings. The result may well be a legible map for many readers, with the allegory keeping things decorous. But the clarity of the imagery keeps the reader at a safe distance.

Harryman, on the other hand, draws her readers into a problematic condition, pleasurable, but quite unsettling. The narrative ends rapidly, in almost screwball fashion, with many complications impinging at once. The collector leaves the room for a phone call. The narrator begins to masturbate in earnest, simultaneously picking up the extension to eavesdrop on the collector. He, it turns out is giving money to anti-art fanatics who want to ban all nudes from public spaces. This will give them the "forbidden pleasure of a black market item and [will] drive the price up." The narrator finds this a bit preposterous, unpredictable, and exciting. The narrative ends with her/him having an orgasm just before the collector hangs up and comes back into the room.

As a representation of a condition beyond gender, the narrative is both visceral and highly speculative. One of the most interesting features is the way Harryman has set this quasi-utopic representation in the midst of some of the conditions of the present that are harsh, tawdry, and, it should be added, illicitly exciting (at least to some bodies). Terrorism, art speculation, pornographic inequities are all yoked into an imagination of gender conditions that would herald a more just, open, and exciting future. Such a darkly dappled paradise is visible as an extension of the present: for readers who want to know where they are now, it makes a much better map than a pure utopia that lives up to its name by being radically separated from existing locales.

EIGHT

An Alphabet of Literary History

A

I will not attempt to determine
the exact import of the promise

that an Author in the present
historical moment, publishing in a critical

format, makes to the Reader; but
I am certain it will appear

to many that I am not
fulfilling the terms of an engagement

thus voluntarily contracted. They who have
been accustomed to the gaudiness and

inane phraseology of many modern critics,
if they persist in reading this

chapter to its conclusion, will, doubtless,
frequently receive impressions of a naive

verbal positivism: as if the act
of writing could always keep its

words particular. Those expecting reference to
uniform discursive terms will be induced

to inquire, by what species of
courtesy these attempts can be permitted

to assume the title of literary,
history, theory, or even of poetry.

B

The concepts are surprisingly portable. What
look at first like **B**oulders marking

the genres, movable only by large
groups in concert, break upon reading

and writing into words, quick gatherings
of air, the slightest social masses:

these never appear in the literary
orreries. Semes? I know not semes.

I ply my needle, ply over
ply. As you word each line,

reader, and examine the lineaments of
the phrases, feel as well the

body reading, its present weather. I
am mad for it to be

in contact with us. But we'd
better skip the finer points or

we won't get a good spot
to watch the march of literature,

a.k.a. the triumph of criticism. We've
missed the first floats already—Look!

the flowers seem so fresh. It
must be because they're kept in

past tense. Little John Milton sat
in the center and sang to

the center things never before attempted
in prose or rhyme. He stuck

in his morally oblique body, and
pulled out an unchangeable ethics, which,

unfortunately, needed gendered guywires to remain
vertical. These thrummed in the wind.

Their lengths were unequal: that's how
iambs were born. They were led

to meaning in mechanzied rituals; but
with the invention first of decorum,

then of style, and finally of
nature, the slaughter became more humane.

They felt as little as possible,
mooing and swishing their tails as

they followed one another up the
curving ramps to the moment of

literary history. Ask your Mama. On
the next float, Goodman Bob found

himself in the forest, where an
unholy host, possibly post-marxian, of syntactic

displacements was boring the heck out
of the (mono)culture, the zeitgeist, Hegel

himself. An owl pushed his glasses
up on his beak and flew

into the dusk, "I knew Hegel;
and you're no Hegel." His pinions

clacked in apogee, disgustedly. "To even
mention Hegel in this context is

unhegelian." He flew across the Atlantic
to the next float, and alit

on a bust of Dante in
a small, second-story flat. On this

float, made entirely of hulled sunflower
seeds, Pound, Bob's uncle, actively courted

circumstance. Pound was not his real
name. He'd tried to write enough

money to buy Europe back from
the ever-more-industrialized hordes who had flooded

it with replicated modern desire. Ezra
was his real name. He'd asked

Dante for money, quite a lot
actually, and now couldn't pay it

back—what's new? He would die
in obliquity, haggling in ideograms, his

vertical sun shut in yellow guidebooks.
Meanwhile, back on the Nowheresville float,

Williams was burning leaves of grass,
trying to avoid the bitter smoke.

He went inside and searched
the refrigerator. The plums were gone. The

cold of verbal construction was delicious
in isolation but the question of

social value remained in abeyance: there
was really nothing to eat. Only

some Rimbaud stuck to the shelves.
"O lilies, O enema-bags!" echoed wanly

in translation. Where were they when
he'd needed them? And which had

he needed? How to tell without
a tradition of seduction and instruction?

C

A Critic came to me and asked, What is language writing? fetching it to
me with full hands. I guess it is a uniform hieroglyphic, sprouting
alike in prose and in verse, in love-sighs and guerilla acting-out
from under administered language deep in a million Broca's areas
as told to any one tongue.

Or I guess it is the birth of post-industrial code-splicing from a shoal of
territorial barks before any one dog had had enough. This process
gripped down and began to awaken just after the death of Hamlet's
father in a material downpour, not just poison in the ear but coins

embossed with sovereigns and one dollar bills with pictures of
buildings and ozone-depleting air-conditioning systems but if you
don't keep the windows rolled down you can't hear the words of
the song traveling through the dark of the electoral forest.

In language writing any president of any body may name a cloud a
whale a whale a cloud a whale a whale a cloud a cloud. If so, she
should be complimented, complemented, and called on it.

D

A woman a
human a man
a person an
American an eagle
a tiger a
pussycat a recipient
a proDucer a
reader a writer

E

Before I writE
I have complete
autonomy to write
what I like

Afterwards you
have to
live with
those words

F

Yes, the poetry journals had been right. It was time for him to set out on his
journey eastward; panoptical terminology was general all over these literary
states. It was falling on every grade level of the dark central plain, falling
softly upon the Bog of Language Writing, and, farther eastward, softly falling
through the dark, mutinous, Freudian vacation hours.

G

For the record: Speech is writin**G**,
writin**G** speech. That is the lesson

the body waits to hear with
every word it reads. The voice

which might still be Whitman's emerges
from the wash of static on

the old wax cylinder and names
America the center of equal daughters,

equal sons, perennial with the earth,
with Freedom, Law and Love, and

Ginsberg noted the Brooklyn accent of
Love. But is it still really

Walt? On it rise solid growths
that offset the growths of pine

and cedar and hemlock and liveoak
and locust and hickory and limetree

and cottonwood and tuliptree and cactus
and wildvine and tamarind and persimmon.

Tangles as wild as any canebrake.
Forests coated with transparent ice and

icicles hanging from the boughs crackling
in the wind. Sides and peaks

of mountains. Pasturage sweet and free
as savannah or upland or prairie.

With flights and songs and screams
that answer those of the wildpigeon

and highhold and orchard-oriole and coot
and surf-duck and redshouldered-hawk and fish-hawl

and white-ibis and indian-hen and cat-owl
and water-pheasant and qua-bird and pied-sheldrake

and blackbird and mockingbird and buzzard
and condor and night-heron and eagle.

So many names to memorize! One's
own the hardest of all. And

they hardly fit into the landscape
anymore, maintained only by a kind

of secular piety. Walt! I have
an announcement! Our wide, semi-civilized Lethe

leads to Newark, that landfill-haunted, not-so-residential
bedroom the majority of travelers fly

above, thumbing through the inflight mags
while waiting for juice! It was

one of many places the war
came home, in bodybags, in bodies,

in lines separating classes. Ask Baraka.
A late fall sun drapes a

momentary eulogy over the Whitman Bridge:
America, brawny-limbed projection embracing its mapper,

individual bodies selected for universal love.
But he skipped the rest of

"America": "A grand, sane, towering, seated
Mother, / Chair'd in the adamant of

Time." Perhaps there wasn't enough wax.
What's new? Very few mothers get

chairs. The Atlantic coast stretched long
and the Pacific coast stretched long

but it easily stretched with them
north or south. It spanned between

them east to west, quotation changing
instantly to writing and back. The

continent is waiting for its connectors.

H

Criticism is the pain I **H**ear
when I name what I say.

Then I have to wait.

I

I didn't want to write
a poem.
I wanted to speak
my mind.

J & K

Ladies and gentlemen
crouching for employment
reading what other readers
have thought they've read

or like a congregation
listening to Latin
and en**J**oying the sense
of a communal rite

croo**K**ed figures of common sense
and deferred reunificiation
sending thousands to class,
fed, sheltered, evaluated.

L

Let the bird with most PR
On the sole American Tree
Herald glad and trumpet be:

Poet and critic both are dead,
Fled in mutual fame from hence.

Let us now ring aura's knell:
I'll begin it. Ding! Dong! Bell!

M

O for a Muse of fire that would take
the shuttle bus from Gare-du-Nord
to the brightest heaven of invention
printed in Material form
read by Material readers.

N

"I Never read the book you gave me twentyfive years ago. I want
you to know that I have Now and that it is remarkable."
—William Carlos Williams to Charles Reznikoff

O

Can this line hold the vasty theory of France?
Or may we cram within this compact noise
the very O of poems that did affright
the air of APR and NPR (not to mention the NYRB)?

Since masterful theory may attest
in transposed light the luscious sun,
then let me, a cipher to this great accompt
on your practico-poetic phobias work.

Suppose within the girdle of the next quatrain
are now confined two mighty literary movements
whose poly-headed and abutting fronts
the perilous narrow years spin quite differently:

The Objectivists, in the marginalized trunks,
speaking new American to one another as if to a crowd of energized
        workers
and the language writers, wearing nothing but the opaque materiality
        of words,
passing notes a bird would sing if birds would only read.

P

Language writing beckons
        as modernism beckoned.
                Critical genealogy is a kind

of art **P**rose,
>a sort of **P**oetics,
>>even

a **P**oem, since the lines it rewrites are new lines
>read by readers
>>heretofore unaddressed,

unmarked—
>since their eyes
>>are focused on new media
(even though formally these were unaccredited.)

No poem is made up entirely of language—since
the channels it leases are always conduits
>formerly
>>unarticulated. A

world lost,
>a world unarticulated,
>>beckons to new genres
and no poetic value (eternal) is so unnegotiable as the memory
of value lost

Q & R

Q. Have you ever worked as a:
>textile worker
>smelter
>paint production
>shoe production
>leather production
>farmer
>sailor or fisherman
>chemist
>**R**adiologist
>wood fiber production

T, U, V

When we **T**raduce Tradition and produce
group feedback, hunting and pecking for

private truth on public screens, think
that you see words in lines,

moving in the world that is
moving with your Use. Didn't your

eyes just moVe from left to
right and down? Or was that

a pulse of common time beating
in our minds? For it's your

words that now must deck my
words, raise them and celebrate them,

close their eyes and simply read
them, carry them here, drop them

there, saxifrage our flower anticipating space.
Admit me chorus to this history.

W

I'm going out to clean the Pierian Spring;
I'll only stop when all career lyricisms
are spread out on the word-tables, leaching
to the pocked sidewalks where some readers are in bed
by noon staring at their shoes.—You Write too.

X & Y

I'm going out to grow loaves of grass above the Peorian aquafer: I'll lead the
calves away from their mother tongue, so that all identity poetics, including
aerobic, fleXible, transnational English rich as a sauced clam on a hill, will
open to the menu's who's-who, the cars' parade, the words outside the poem.
You eat too.

Z

I heard a fly buzZ when I wrote.

Notes

A: William Wordsworth, "Preface to the Lyrical Ballads."

B: William Shakespeare, *Hamlet*; Ezra Pound, *The Cantos*; Walt Whitman, "Song of Myself"; Percy Shelley, "The Triumph of Life"; John Milton, *Paradise Lost*; Mother Goose; Langston Hughes, *Ask Your Mama*; Nathaniel Hawthorne, "Young Goodman Brown"; William Carlos Williams, "This is just to say"; Arthur Rimbaud, "Album Called Zutique, 'Lily.'"

C: "Song of Myself"; *Hamlet*; Williams, "By the road to the contagious hospital"; William Stafford, "Travelling Through the Dark."

F: James Joyce, "The Dead."

G: John Keats, "Ode on a Grecian Urn"; Whitman, *Leaves of Grass*, 1st edition, introduction; John Ashbery, "Daffy Duck in Hollywood"

J & K: Shakespeare, *Henry V*; Rimbaud, "The Drunken Boat."

L: Shakespeare, "The Phoenix and the Turtle"; *The Merchant of Venice*.

M, O, and P: Shakespeare, *Henry V*

Q: Insurance questionnaire.

R: Williams, "The Descent."

T, U, V: Williams, "Three Sonnets"; "A Sort of a Song."

W, X & Y: Robert Frost, "You Come Too."

Z: Emily Dickinson, 465.

NINE

A False Account of Talking with Frank O'Hara and Roland Barthes in Philadelphia

"And don't worry about your lineage, poetic or natural"
—Frank O'Hara

I really shouldn't have been doing it. I had a book to write, poems that needed care and breaking apart and confidence, I wasn't getting much exercise, and of course there was real life, family, teaching, the out-of-date inspection sticker on the Honda . . . Anyway, in spite of all this, and because of it too, no doubt, I found myself in front of the tube, in a curious state of wakeful paralysis. Never had the remote control felt more present, not exactly flesh of my flesh, but anticipatory, fateful, quirky. I noticed that it had many more buttons than I was used to. I had just been glancing through another boring human-interest piece about "The Information Highway" ten minutes previously: five hundred channels soon, marketing conundrums, visionary entrepreneurs. Then I put two and two together. I was dreaming. I didn't need to count the buttons: there would be five hundred.

This was nice. I never, or say very rarely, get to control my dreams. But here was the vaguely magic clicker and here I was, too, on the couch in the den. Things might be a little deterministic finally, but it was better than nothing. I pushed 136.

Well, life is full of nonsurprises, even in dreams. 136 was an ad for Roy Rogers flame-broiled burgers. A young, vaguely Italian-American, but mostly nondescript male model had just come up an escalator into heaven a space of uniform brightness and lots of carbon-dioxide smoke. It was tacky; it *had* to be tacky or it would have caused Fundamentalist-Trouble to use the afterlife for commercial purposes—such blatant ones, that is. Escalators connoting not just painless and progressive death, but automatic heavenly transcendence as well. Hadn't this stage set been used recently in some movies? I'd seen the trailers, so I knew they dealt in white suits, slight overexposure,

Just to make sure: the title of this chapter refers to O'Hara's "A True Account of Talking to the Sun on Fire Island," which in turn refers to Mayazovsky's "An Extraordinary Adventure."

soft focus, and smoke: heaven was personalized, caring technology that led the simple soul to mild corporate advancement. This particular Roy Rogers ad I'd seen a couple of times already. They were about to work in something about open-flame broiling and hell. It was all meant to be disarmingly goofy, but virtuously neutral and tasty.

I pushed 137. At first I thought I hadn't. The buttons were quite close together and the screen looked basically the same: same escalator, same space full of soft white billows. But the next second I saw that this was something else entirely: there were Roland Barthes and Frank O'Hara. They both had pencil-thin William Powell moustaches. The rhythm was diffuse; in fact, nothing was happening. This was no ad. Wait. They were talking, strolling slowly along, stirring up the white smoke just a bit, the camera following them, keeping them centered. What camera? Never mind. I couldn't quite hear. I pushed the volume.

"A dune buggy brought you here."

"And a laundry truck for you."

"And I see you have one of these as well," Barthes gestured to the halo of white smoke that lay above his head, touching it lightly as if he were touching his hair after he'd combed it. "Oh god," said O'Hara. "That." He waved his hand over his head, trying to shoo away an annoyance. His halo reformed. It was pencil-thin. "At least we aren't wearing togas or something." They were both dressed in slacks and alligator shirts. I pushed the volume up some more. They looked toward me a second, then back to each other.

"So. We're supposed to read," O'Hara said.

"Yes, that's the script, it seems. A pity we never heard of each other. A curator and a poet, interesting combination. Although, Frank, I think it's just as well we never met. You would have found my circle a bit boring, perhaps. I did eventually, I'm afraid. We had a little power, but not all that much money."

"Would you have minded this, I wonder? Shall I?" O'Hara held a sheet of typing paper.

"Please."

"The Critic. I cannot possibly think of you other than you are: the assassin of my orchards." O'Hara looked up from the page: "It's early work."

"It's quite alright, Frank, early work is charming when it's light enough."

"You lurk there in the shadows, meting out conversation like Eve's first confusion between penises and snakes."

"You know, my students used to mix up penises and phalluses: it got tiresome."

"Oh be droll, be jolly, and be temperate! Do not frighten me more than you have to! I must live forever."

Barthes waited.

"That's it," O'Hara said. "For that one."

"But the poem gives me no offense: you must know, I was never 'The Critic.' Go ahead, live forever! You must admit, it's slightly comic. And anyway, you were flirting there more than attacking, am I right? Another thing: you were a bit of the prophet: I was 'droll, jolly, and temperate'—at least on the good days—and those were the days I wrote." He scuffed his foot in the smoke: it billowed up to his white-clad knee. "Jolly? No, not jolly. And not really droll, either. But, temperate, yes."

"Ah, Sir Roland, when I write it, you mustn't take 'jolly' to mean jolly. But perhaps your appetite for falseness was different from mine. All my words were as false as false eyelashes: but of course I'm looking directly at you when I say them. So you'll have to kiss semiology goodbye. On the eyelashes, of course. Zukofsky, a poet I never read, Louis Zukofsky. He was a formalist like even you wouldn't have believed, a formalist and, finally, a bit of a whiner—but don't you think all formalists, deep down, are whiners?"

Barthes shrugged. "Ah yes, but there's spontaneous whining as well."

O'Hara went on. "Zukofsky believed in the words themselves: yawn—now that's a 'word,' isn't it? As if going to bed with the dictionary was a joy forever, or even for the first five minutes. He wrote one nice thing, though. He tells a joke in a poem, it's only a few lines, and even there he's too coy, but, still, it's a good joke: the sailor's on the operating table, for a hernia or something. The surgeon sees his cock—Zukofsky calls it something else of course—and when the sailor comes to, the surgeon comments on the graceful message that he had read tattooed on the sailor's phallus—is that what you called it in those seminars?"

"No, no: penis, penis. Phallus points to the universal ineffability around which all the differential structures of language, the social hierarchies . . . But, please, get to the punchline."

"So the surgeon comments on the graceful message that he had read tattooed on the sailor's *penis*—so what's with 'phallus' then? Sorry, onward to the punchline: the graceful message on the sailor's penis: the word SWAN. The sailor says, 'SWAN? SWAN? What SWAN? No, that was SASKATCHEWAN.' Well, all my pretty swans are Saskatchewans, if you know what I mean."

"So you liked the pretty falsenesses that lead directly to the body's outrageous truths. Then, I wonder; you might have agreed with this: may I?" Barthes opened a paperback.

"Please."

"Contemporary poetry is *a regressive semiological system*. We talked like that too. At least in the seminars. . . . It tries to transform the sign back into meaning: its ideal, ultimately, would be to reach not the meaning of words, but the meaning of things themselves. . . . Hence the essentialist ambitions of poetry . . . of all those who use speech, poets are the least . . ."

"Wait! How about this? We join the animals not when we fuck or shit not when tear falls but when staring into the light . . ." O'Hara inserted a thin pause. ". . . we think. Oh, I don't know. I don't buy it myself. David Smith made me say it."

"What can I say, Frank? We said a lot of things when we got enthused. I'll continue. Of all those who use speech—should I have said, 'of all animals who use speech'?—poets are the least formalist, for they are the only ones who believe that the meaning of the words is only a form, with which they, being realists, cannot be content. This is why our modern poetry always asserts itself as a murder of language."

"Thanks a lot."

"I know. A murder of language, a kind of spatial, tangible analogue of silence—I'm afraid we were a bit overfond of those poetic phrases. Poetry occupies a position which is the reverse of that of myth: myth is a semiological system which has the pretension of transcending itself into a factual system; poetry is a semiological system which has the pretension of contracting itself into an essential system. That was in *Mythologies*. It, also, was early work."

"Well I'll tell you. What I was aiming to make direct contact with was not the *meaning* of things but bodies—very particular ones. I hated poetic phrases, by the way. Here, how about this. Here's from 'Personism: A Manifesto.' May I?" The typing paper was folded in half, with a number of circular stains on it from bottoms of glasses. O'Hara unfolded it.

"Please."

"I don't believe in god—and I still don't." O'Hara kicked at the smoke. "This smoke is *cheap*. I know I wasn't Fred Astaire, or Ballanchine, or even Gene Kelly, for god's sake, but, still, I always appreciated genuine surfaces. Well, what is one to do?—*now*, I mean. As I was saying. I don't believe in god, so I don't have to make elaborately sounded structures. But Zukofsky didn't believe in god either, so maybe I was wrong. Well, it sounded good when I said it. He's a little scary, Zukofsky. I don't even like rhythm, assonance, all that stuff. You just go on your nerve. I'll skip a bunch. His dreaming angel," he nodded at me, "has only moderately fast handwriting.

"How can you really care whether anyone gets it, or gets what it means, or if it improves them. Improves them for what? For death? I'm skipping, skipping. As for measure and other technical apparatus, that's just common sense: if you're going to buy a pair of pants you want them to be tight enough so everyone will want to go to bed with you. I still can't skip that. Personism has nothing to do with philosophy, it's all art. Skipping. To give you a vague idea, one of its minimal aspects is to address itself to one person (other than the poet himself), thus evoking overtones of love without destroying love's life-giving vulgarity. It puts the poem squarely between the poet and the person, Lucky Pierre style, and the poem is correspondingly gratified. The poem is at last between two persons instead of two pages. In all modesty I confess that it may be the death of literature as we know it. Although now that I'm here—*this* is the death of literature as I knew it."

"But we can talk," said Barthes, "and we have this frozen dreaming worthy on his couch here to write it down for us."

I tried to interrupt him and say that I could talk, that it was *my* dream anyway and not him at all, that I wanted to make a point about the differences between a career made of writing with the stuff of everyday life and one built around reading it—suggestively, authoritatively—but fading finally through growing paralysis of desire stilled in the middle of overly legible maps. But it was one of those dreams where your vocal chords are helpless. I stared at him without gesture. My left hand felt the clicker. My right hand, I noticed, was forming letters with a pen.

"That's an old trick," Barthes said, "saying that you can't say something but inventing a figure to say what it is you can't say. I like those old tricks. There would hardly be any literature without them. And not much writing, either, to tell the truth. Isn't that a distinction you're trying to keep in focus? Don't forget. No, no writing at all, really, without such sleights of time. Foreshortenings, nostalgias, longings. With every letter, almost. One might say that they are the heart of the joke. Don't worry, I won't tell anyone."

"When you say *myth*," said O'Hara, "—you didn't read Duncan or Olson, did you? Robert Duncan, Charles Olson? God, you couldn't read two lines of those guys without Venus or Osiris coming on to you. Wagner was *okay*, I suppose, but after a very little while . . ."

"No, I certainly didn't mean the gods. Myth is this." And he kicked the carbon-dioxide smoke. "And especially that," pointing over to the smoke-and-escalator of 136. "The heavenly Roy Rogers flame-broiled burger: as tasty a myth as I could imagine. Shall I be ponderous—as ponderous as one can be in all this smoke—and define: the bourgeois myth of a natural world. And what's more natural than the supernatural made totally consumable? But Charles Olson, Robert Duncan? I'm afraid American poetry never caught my attention, though those two sound interesting, actually. I heard about the Beats, Allen Ginsberg, Kerouac. Were you . . . ?"

"Give me a break, I was never a beatnik. Maybe the best minds of Allen's generation were destroyed, what can I say? If you had to have a *movement* so you could experience life, that's a problem, wouldn't you say?"

"But an individual life is little more than a punchline."

"Maybe. Maybe not. Allen was sweet when he wasn't being the Poet. I was never the Poet, either, if that's what you were thinking of when you wrote *Mythologies*. No, you really must know my work. May I?"

"But of course." Barthes reached down and scooped up some smoke. He let it flow through his fingers and watched it carefully while O'Hara read from sheets of typing paper.

"A Step Away From Them. It's my lunch hour, so I go for a walk among the hum-colored cabs."

"I'm sorry?"

"Hum-colored cabs."

"For a moment, I thought it was 'ham.'"

"Hum-colored. First, down the sidewalk where laborers feed their dirty glistening torsos sandwiches and Coca-Cola, with yellow helmets on."

"Do you miss food?—cooking I should say."

"Not really. First, down the sidewalk where laborers feed their dirty glistening torsos sandwiches and Coca-Cola, with yellow helmets on. They protect them from falling bricks, I guess. Then onto the avenue where skirts are flipping above heels and blow up over grates. The sun is hot, but the cabs stir up the air. I look at bargains in wristwatches. There are cats playing in sawdust. On to Times Square, where the sign blows smoke over my head, and higher the waterfall pours lightly. A Negro stands in a doorway with a toothpick, languorously agitating."

"Languorously agitating: Frank, I detect a poetic phrase—even an elaborately sounded structure."

"It is nice, isn't it? Languorously agitating. A blonde chorus girl clicks: he smiles and rubs his chin. Everything suddenly honks: it is 12:40 of a Thursday. Neon in daylight is a great pleasure, as Edwin Denby would write, as are light bulbs in daylight. I stop for a cheeseburger at JULIET'S CORNER. Guilietta Masina, wife of Federico Fellini, *è bell' attrice*. And chocolate malted. A lady in foxes on such a day puts her poodle in a cab. There are several Puerto Ricans on the avenue today, which makes it beautiful and warm."

Barthes suddenly clenched his fist. Smoke squirted from between his fingers. "Ah, Mr. American Imperial Artist, you were so happy, in your walks, in your world."

"Well, I don't know: First Bunny died, then John Latouche, then Jackson Pollock. But is the earth as full as life was full, of them?"

"And you believed in art triumphing over death!"

"Of course. It has so far, hasn't it? And one has eaten and one walks, past the posters for BULLFIGHT and the Manhattan Storage Warehouse, which they'll soon tear down. I used to think they had the Armory Show there. A glass of papaya juice and back to work. My heart is in my pocket, it is Poems by Pierre Reverdy."

"How did that last part go?"

"First Bunny died, then John Latouche, then Jackson Pollock. But is the earth as full as life was full, of them?"

"Bunny?"

"And one has eaten and one walks . . . Bunny Lang. Violet R. Lang, Poets Theatre, Cambridge, Massachusetts."

"Bunny, and not Jack?"

"Nobody called him Jack. 'Jack Pollock.' It has a certain ring, but it's the wrong ring."

"Were you writing there as curator or poet?"

"Neither."

"You can't really say that."

"I did, though. And one walks past the posters for BULLFIGHT and the Manhattan Storage Warehouse, which they'll soon tear down. I used to think they had the Armory Show there. A glass of papaya juice and back to work. My heart is in my pocket, it is Poems by Pierre Reverdy."

"Lucky man! Lucky Pierre I guess you say! When was that? '60? '62?"

"1956."

"1956: even luckier—for you, that is. We'd been in Indo-China, Algiers. You could aim to live in a world without other countries except Europe and simply be cosmopolitan. Curatorial without having to worry about grants or wallspace. Cabs, Puerto Ricans, Negroes, chocolate malteds, Jackson Pollock, weather, time: perfectly innocent appetite, spiced by the view into the abyss of death. You trigger my melancholy. Listen, this was me, walking in my world: If, for instance, I take a walk in Spain—you never walked under an 'If, for instance,' am I right? Well, I always did. It gained me a big audience, but so many of them were *students*, finally. If, for instance, I take a walk in Spain, in the Basque country, I may well notice in the houses an architectural unity, a common style, which leads me to acknowledge the Basque house as a definite ethnic product . . . it does not provoke me into naming it, except if I think to insert it into a vast picture of a rural habitat. But if I am in the Paris region and I catch a glimpse, at the end of the rue Gambetta or the rue Jean-Jaurès, of a natty white chalet with red tiles, dark brown half-timbering, an asymmetrical roof and a wattle-and-daub front, I feel as if I were personally receiving an imperious injunction to name this object a Basque chalet: or even better, to see it as the very essence of *basquity*. . . . And the adhomination is so frank that I feel this chalet has just been created on the spot, *for me* . . . without any trace of the history which has caused it.

"For this interpellent speech is at the same time a frozen speech: at the moment of reaching me, it suspends itself, turns away and assumes the look of a generality: it stiffens, it makes itself look neutral and innocent. . . . This is a kind of *arrest*, in both the physical and legal sense of the term. I hated being called like that. The details became so clear after awhile. Imagine reading where you know the sense *perfectly*, yet you couldn't touch the world."

"That's why I liked the movies and Ballanchine and de Kooning and my friends. And Rachmaninoff."

"Reading got to be such a chore, Frank. After I got perfect at it, I liked to read perversely: 'the obtuse meaning,' I called it. But I really wanted it to stop altogether. It was very restful not to know a language. All codes are vulgar. I did get it to a certain point—here. No codes here at all." He sighed as he showed O'Hara a small picture. "My mother as a small child. You haven't seen her here, have you?"

"No, I've only seen you, as a matter of fact. But, you know, I liked walking under a—what did you say?—under a 'for instance.' Here's another one about the Manhattan Storage Warehouse: Une Journée de Juillet." The top of the page was torn. "Nuts. You know I never memorized anything. Let's see: it was hot, lots of sun, tar melting underfoot, sweat, I was walking through crowds. Okay, here: The sun beams on my buttocks as I outdistance the crowd. For a moment I enter the cavernous vault and its deadish cold."

"I understand the cavernous vault you entered; I entered it myself every time I read something, and most especially every time I looked at a photograph. Life consisted of these little touches of solitude."

"That's only the set-up. I suck off every man in the Manhattan Storage & Warehouse Co. Then, refreshed, again to the streets! to the generous sun and the vigorous heat of the city—July 12, 1955."

"But . . . May I ask you a personal question?"

"They're the only kind I like."

"Perhaps he should mute the volume, don't you think?"

"Oh let him hear. I *want* him to. He's just making all this up anyway. We're both perfectly safe—which is a drag. All that gets left is *the works*; the moments are missing." A white smoke tear drifted down his cheek. "Okay! Okay! So it's smoke." O'Hara glared upward. He took his typescripts and fanned the air above his head vigorously, dispersing the smoke of his halo. But it kept reforming.

Barthes sighed. "I suppose you're right: we're safe. Well, don't let this sound naive. But the referent itself?"

"Those men in there, you mean? The Manhattan Storage Warehouse?"

"There is—sorry, there was—a science of the single body that I tried all my life to write. The pleasure of the text. Society was a vast code and one could stir the grids with one's sentences, but I wanted to be able to write a body exactly. You seemed to have had pleasure, and then to have written. Or to have written in anticipation of pleasure. But you wrote in the present, not *as* the present. You didn't try to make writing *be* pleasure, did you? You didn't try to *write* pleasure."

"I was happy and I wrote. I stopped, you know."

"I wrote to be happy. I couldn't stop. I never was."

The smoke had grown thicker. As they reached this broken symmetry, the screen grew totally white a moment.

"That's such an easy ending. It's like this damn smoke. Contemporary cultural information has to be *challenged*: just reading it or celebrating one's navigation among its shoals won't do." I heard myself saying this.

They waved a window in the center of the smoke and peered out. "This is all *fiction*, isn't it?" They were speaking in unison now. They had their arms over one another's shoulder, and were looking right out at me. They had italicized "fiction."

Barthes went on, "And not all that perfect fiction, either: the verbs of saying, the physical props. Not to mention the plot."

"Perhaps he needs to *revise*," O'Hara said. They laughed.

I felt the buttons of the remote control were less under my control. There weren't as many as I had thought. The smoke settled back down to knee-height. "Neither of us *ever* resorted to fiction, let alone allegorical fiction. That's why we're heroic—you for the poets, Frank," said Barthes, "—and you for the critics, Roland," said O'Hara.

"That's why both your careers came to the impasses that they did," I said. "That's why neither of you were language writers."

"Please, do not play the goat," said Barthes. "I'd hardly call our careers 'impasses.' You must remember that you're asleep so anything you say is more or less upside down. You'd never possibly say anything like that when you were awake. Mille sabors! Language writers hate fiction. Even we know that much."

"Come on, he's not sleeping," O'Hara said. "Look at him looking out the window thinking what to write next. 'What are those fuzzy things out there— *trees*? Well, I'm tired of them.'" He turned to Barthes: "I'm quoting Williams's grandmother. Sort of."

"No, *I'm* quoting Williams's grandmother," I said. "Williams, I mean."

"You can *quote* it, but you can only *say* it when you're dead or dying."

"Williams didn't."

"You Americans are obsessed with self-fashioned lineage, aren't you?" Barthes said. "It must be the New World." He mused, "'Language writing,' 'Roy Rogers flame burgers'—why privilege any one bead of the necklace? It's beautiful, but it can choke." He was wearing a long necklace of smoke beads. He grabbed it and started twirling it in front of his chest. The smoke beads shot off slowly, dispersing. He tried to eat one of the detached enlarging beads. O'Hara elbowed him and shot him a look that said, "It won't be satisfying."

O'Hara gestured out of the screen. "He wants to conjure up the birth of language writing from personism and the heroic decodings of taste—god knows why."

"That means he *is* asleep. Upside down."

"He's drawn us out of his narrow cathexes—500 channels my eye. So now, Croque Monsieur, you've got to put in the date, just like I did: May 13th, I still keep track of these things, 1994—lucky *dog. Touch* those keys—Friday, the whole schmear: 2:30 P.M., right?"

"Tonerre du Brest! What if he rewrites? Hegel, et cetera, et cetera. It will be much later. The accuracy will go."

"Let him."

"I predict—though I'm in no position to—he aims for 'an elaborately sounded structure.'"

"Let him try."

NOTES

Chapter Two

1. "Formal" is an easily misleading word in poetic contexts. In mainstream parlance, "form" means inherited form: iambic pentameter, rhyme, sonnets. In language writing, "form" is opposed to inherited forms. It is often programmatic or experimental: writing forty-five chapters of forty-five sentences each as Lyn Hejinian does in *My Life* (2d ed. [Los Angeles: Sun & Moon Press, 1987]); writing only the first five words of every sentence as I do in "Chronic Meanings" (in *Virtual Reality* [New York: Roof Press, 1993]); using a word list, as Charles Bernstein does in "I and the " (in *The Sophist* [Los Angeles: Sun & Moon Press, 1987]); specifying that "I" and names of political leaders occur once a page, as Barrett Watten does in *Progress* (New York: Roof Press, 1985).
2. *The New Princeton Encyclopedia of Poetry and Poetics*, Alex Preminger and T.V.F. Brogan, eds. (Princeton: Princeton University Press, 1993), 675–76. Note the difference in name: language writing; language poetry. I discuss the difficulties with the movement's name in a moment.
3. As a further problem confronting natural readers, these claims are often in French. See David Simpson's *Romanticism, Nationalism, and the Revolt Against Theory* (Chicago: University of Chicago Press, 1993) for discussion of the ways espousal of common sense and attacks on theory have become intertwined with nationalism.
4. The former comment comes from Silliman's contribution to "The Politics of Poetry," in *L=A=N=G=U=A=G=E* 9/10 (October 1979), n.p.; the latter can be found in "Spicer's Language" (*Writing/Talks*, ed. Bob Perelman [Carbondale: Southern Illinois University Press, 1985], 167).
5. Ron Silliman, *Tjanting* (Berkeley: The Figures, 1981), 109. Thanks to Tom Vogler for calling my attention to this sentence.
6. This was in a letter written in 1994.
7. Zukofsky's *"A"-24*, a two-hundred-page vocal score for four speaking voices set by his wife to Handel harpsichord music, concludes his life-epic *"A."*
8. Transcripts of some of the talks can be found in the *Talks* issue of *Hills* magazine (6/7) and in *Writing/Talks*, ed. Bob Perelman.
9. The sense of a deliberate critical project has been carried out more recently in *Poetics Journal*, each of whose issues is organized around a given topic such as "Public & Private Language," "Women and Language," or "Postmodernism?"
10. Lewis's article appeared in the October/November 1990 issue of *Poets & Writers Magazine*; the letters appeared in the January/February 1991 issue. The letter and poem quoted here are by Carol F. Ra.
11. Robert Cooperman, ibid.
12. *Politics & Poetic Value*, ed. Robert von Hallberg (Chicago: University of Chicago Press, 1987). The early version was *Critical Inquiry* 13, no. 3 (Spring 1987).

13. *In The American Tree: Language Realism Poetry*, ed. Ron Silliman (Orono, ME: National Poetry Foundation, 1986). *"Language" Poetries: An Anthology*, ed. Douglas Messerli (New York: New Directions, 1987).

14. Silliman called a smaller anthology, published prior to *In The American Tree*, "Realism: An Anthology of 'Language' Writing" (*Ironwood* 20 [Fall 1982]). In his introduction, Silliman gives a detailed history of the term "language," 62–70.

15. Silliman, *American Tree*, pp. xx–xxi.

16. "The impetus for this anthology was two previous anthologies: Ron Silliman's *In the American Tree* and Douglas Messerli's *'Language' Poetries*. None of the poets included here appeared in those books." *The Art of Practice: 45 Contemporary Poets*, ed. Dennis Barone and Peter Ganick (Elwood, CT: Potes and Poets Press, 1994), xiv.

17. While in a sense this is true—technically the collection was a double issue of the magazine—the desire to avoid authoritarian definition seems obvious. "We are the generation of writers that grew up with a photograph of the earth tacked to our walls. . . . All boundaries or clear definitions of identity are eroded, active and blurred." Peter Gizzi, "Foreword," "Writing from the New Coast: Presentation," *O.blēk* 12 (Spring/Fall 1993), n.p. [i–ii].

18. Rae Armantrout, *Precedence* (Providence: Burning Deck, 1985), 12.

19. *Necromance* (Los Angeles: Sun & Moon Press, 1991), 39.

20. David Melnick, *Pcoet* (San Francisco: G.A.W.K, 1975), n.p.

21. From "A Short Word on My Work," in $L=A=N=G=U=A=G=E$ 1, no. 1 (February 1978), n.p.

22. *Men in Aida* (Berkeley: Tuumba Press, 1983), 1.

    The Greek from which Melnick shapes his English can be transliterated as follows:

> Mēnin ēade, Thēa, Pēlēiadeo Achilleus
> oulomenēn, hē muri Achaiois alge ethēke,
> pollas d'ifthimous psouxas Aidi proiapsen
> haeroön, autous de heloria teuxe kunessin
> oionoisi te pasi, Dios d' etelēeto boulē,
> ex hu dēa ta prota diastētēn erisante
> Atrēidēs te anax andron kai dios Achilleus.

23. Bruce Andrews, *Give Em Enough Rope* (Los Angeles: Sun & Moon Press, 1987), 27.

24. From "The Town of He" in *Blue Book* (Great Barrington: The Figures, 1988), 195.

25. Ron Silliman, *What* (Great Barrington: The Figures, 1988), 40.

26. An early poem such as "Berkeley" in *This* 5, seems specifically designed to destroy any reading which would produce a unified subject. The poem consists of a hundred or so first-person sentences whose mechanical aspect—each starts with "I"—makes them impossible to unite: "I want to redeem myself / I can shoot you / I've no idea really / I should say it is not a mask / I must remember another time / I don't want to know you / I'm not dressed / I had to take the risk / I did look / I don't care what you make of it / I am outside in the sun / I still had what was mine / I will stay here and die / I was reinforced in this opinion / I flushed it down the toilet / I collapsed into my chair / I forgot the place, sir"—etc.

27. Kit Robinson, *The Champagne of Concrete* (Elmwood, CT: Potes & Poets Press, 1990), 42–43.
28. *Balance Sheet* (New York: Roof, 1993), 62–63.
29. See Chapter 4 for extensive discussion of this term.
30. "The Wide Road," excerpt published in *Everyday Life*, no. 2 (August 1988), ed. Chris and George Tysh, 2–3.
31. Roland Barthes, *S/Z*, trans. Richard Miller (New York: Hill & Wang, 1974), 4.
32. Altieri's criticism, to recall an earlier point, was focused on the chimerical freedom of the reader. However, the possibilities that poems can suggest to a writer are quite a different matter.
33. Although, as I remember, none of us had many academic papers lying around at the time.
34. These phrases are from an article by David Bromige on an Objectivist conference in Paris.
35. Bob Perelman, "The First Person," *Hills* 6/7.
36. Barrett Watten, *1–10* (San Francisco: This Press, 1980).
37. Bob Perelman, *a.k.a.* (Great Barrington: The Figures, 1984).
38. in *Hills* 4 and 5.
39. "The young are masters at the art of writing before having lived. They search for sentiments to accommodate to their vocabulary rather than words to express their feelings and their ideas" is a remark by Davray often quoted by Pound (in French). It makes an interesting side-note. Such a dismissal of language as a juvenile playground is still the foundation of many attacks on language writing. Lyn Hejinian's statement reverses Pound's valuation of language and experience: "Writing develops subjects that mean the words we have for them" (in "The Rejection of Closure," *Poetics Journal* 4 (1984): 140.
40. *Social Text* 19/20 (Fall 1988): 261–75.
41. Andre Breton, *Manifestoes of Surrealism*, trans. Richard Seaver and Helen R. Lane (Ann Arbor: University of Michigan Press, 1972), 14.
42. The ideology of poetic voice precludes such response: a poet's voice, if validated, is difficult to appropriate—it is a bastion of aura. However, the range of voice poems tends to be small.

Chapter Three

1. Philip Whalen, *On Bear's Head* (New York: Harcourt, Brace & World, 1969). For Susan Howe's readings on Dickinson, see *My Emily Dickinson* (Berkeley, CA: North Atlantic Books, 1985), and *The Birth-Mark: Unsettling the Wilderness in American Literary History* (Hanover, NH: Wesleyan University Press, 1993), 131–54. For Marta Werner's, see "Divinations: Emily Dickinson's Scriptive Economies," in *A Poetics of Criticism*, ed. Juliana Spahr, Mark Wallace, Kristin Prevallet, and Pam Rehm (Buffalo: Leave Books. 1994), 87–96, and *Emily Dickinson's Open Folios: Scenes of Reading, Surfaces of Writing* (Ann Arbor: University of Michigan Press, 1995).
2. Paul de Man, "Literary History and Literary Modernity," in *Blindness and Insight: Essays in the Rhetoric of Contemporary Criticism* (Minneapolis: University of Minnesota Press, 1983), 142–65.

3. Writing of Schoenberg, Adorno asserts that "The state of technique appears as a problem in every measure which [the composer] dares to conceive: with every measure technique as a whole demands of him that he do it justice and that he give the single correct answer permitted by technique at any given moment" (36). Thus a particular chord does not have an unvarying meaning: "The diminished seventh chord, which rings false in salon pieces, is correct and full of every possible expression at the beginning of Beethoven's *Sonata opus 111*" (34–35). Theodor W. Adorno, *Philosophy of Modern Music*, trans. Anne G. Mitchell and Wesley V. Blomster (New York: The Seabury Press, 1973).

In "Politics of Theory," Fredric Jameson uses plus and minus signs to indicate whether a given postmodern philosophy is progressive or reactionary. Quoted in Jeffrey T. Nealon, *Double Reading: Postmodernism and Deconstruction* (Ithaca: Cornell University Press: 1993), 133.

4. Basil Bunting, *Collected Poems* (London: Flucrum Press, 1970), 102.

In "Literary History and Literary Modernity," de Man comes very close to Bunting's terms: "Fashion (mode) can sometimes be only what remains of modernity after the impulse has subsided—and this can be almost at once—as it has changed from being an incandescent point in time into a reproduceable cliche," 147.

5. Ron Silliman, "Language, Realism, Poetry," in *In The American Tree*, ed. Ron Silliman (Orono, ME: National Poetry Foundation, 1986), xv.

6. The subsequent writing and publishing activities of Bromige and Mac Low associate them closely with language writing. Palmer and Coolidge are sometimes referred to as language writers: looking at their work formally and at their publishing patterns will not make differentiation very easy.

7. Louis Zukofsky, *Prepositions: The Collected Critical Essays of Louis Zukofsky*, expanded edition (Berkeley: University of California Press, 1981), 14.

8. I discuss this in *The Trouble With Genius* (Berkeley: University of California Press, 1994), 187.

9. *All Stars*, ed. Tom Clark (Santa Fe and New York: Goliard and Grossman, 1972), 251–72.

10. Robert Grenier, "Robert Creeley: *A Quick Graph*"; and "Gertrude Stein: *Lectures in America*," *This* 1 (Iowa City, 1971), n.p.

11. The passage is from Pound's letters: "Objectivity and again objectivity, and expression: no hindside-beforeness, no straddled adjectives (as 'addled mosses dank'), no Tennysonianness of speech; nothing—thing that you couldn't, in some circumstance, in the stress of some emotion, actually say." Pound goes on in favor of real life: "Every literaryism, every book word, fritters away a scrap of the reader's patience, a scrap of his sense of your sincerity." *The Selected Letters of Ezra Pound*, ed. D. D. Paige (New York: New Directions, 1971), 49. Williams's slogan occurs in his *Autobiography* (New York: Random House, 1951), 311.

12. Silliman is quite aware of these ironies concerning speech. He comments on the importance of speech to Olson's poetics and mentions that "Wintry," a poem of Grenier's in the issue, is built around investigation into American-Norwegian dialect. Ibid.

In Silliman's own writing, as the following excerpts from "The Chinese Notebook" should make clear, it was crucial to distance himself from Olson's speech-based poetics:

8. This is not speech. I wrote it.

. . .

22. The page intended to score speech. What an elaborate fiction that seems!

. . .

41. Speech only tells you the speaker.

. . .

137. The concept that the poem "expresses" the poet, vocally or otherwise, is at one with the whole body of thought identified as Capitalist Imperialism.

. . .

The Age of Huts (New York: Roof, 1986), 43, 45, 47, 57.

13. William Carlos Williams, "The Modern Primer," in *The Embodiment of Knowledge*, ed. Ron Loewinsohn (New York: New Directions, 1974), 17. See also "The Author's Introduction" to *The Wedge*, in *The Collected Later Poems of William Carlos Williams* (New York: New Directions, 1963), 5.

14. Charles Olson, "Projective Verse," in *Selected Writings*, ed. Robert Creeley (New York: New Directions, 1975), 17.

15. To anticipate my later discussion of Susan Howe, it is interesting to note that she refers to this passage of Hegel: "The Now that is Night / Time comprehended in Thought" in *Singularities* (Hanover, NH: Wesleyan University Press, 1990), 28. Howe's use of space on the page is in some sense quite similar to Grenier's later holograph pieces, but her commitment to historical specifics—not to mention type!—makes her work much different.

   (For the record, I should note here that I also refer to this Hegel passage. See the title poem in *Face Value*, 13 [New York: Roof Press, 1988]).

16. G.W.F. Hegel, *The Phenomenology of Mind*, trans. J. B. Baille, 2d ed. (London: George Allen & Unwin, 1961), 151–53, 159.

17. An important element in contributing to the impact of *Pieces* is that it breaks down the boundary between public and private. The poems in *For Love* and *Words* may have been based on intense personal experience ("For love—I would / split open your head and put / a candle in / behind the eyes"), but they keep the boundary inviolate. *Pieces*, on the other hand, is also pieces of Creeley's life; *A Day Book* even more so: *Pieces* ends with a description of a three-way sexual encounter; *A Day Book* begins with Creeley and an unnamed woman having sex as his wife is getting the children off to school. This does not make Creeley confessional, however: the difference between his writing and Lowell's or Plath's is that the focus of the poem remains at the level of the syllable; nor are the events presented as subjects for agony. Nevertheless, to ignore Creeley's frankness and to regard his work as purely formal seems a distortion.

18. I am grateful to Peter Quartermain for reminding me that, while praising its immutability, Oppen misquotes Reznikoff's line, changing it to "The girder / itself, among the rubble." Reznikoff's line can be found in *By the Waters of Manhattan: Selected Verse* (New York: New Directions, 1962), 30; Oppen's version in Mary Oppen's "Walking With Charles Reznikoff," in *Charles Reznikoff: Man and Poet*, ed. Milton Hindus (Orono, Maine: National Poetry Foundation, 1984), 79. This

change is discussed by Rachel Blau DuPlessis in "'The familiar / becomes extreme': George Oppen and Silence," and Robert Franciosi in "Reading Reznikoff: Zukofsky and Oppen" both in *North Dakota Quarterly* 55, pp. 18–36, 383–95.

19. Ezra Pound, *The Cantos* (New York: New Directions, 1989), 769.

20. See the discussion of this poem in Chapter Five.

21. *Prepositions: The Collected Critical Essays of Louis Zukofsky*, expanded edition (Berkeley: University of California Press, 1981), 10.

22. But, on the other hand, it is interesting that in the collection *Writing/Talks* Grenier's talk was transcribed—at his insistence—to reflect every noise each speaker made. In such a case, speech was treated like a kind of anthropological music. (See "Language/Site/World" in *Writing/Talks*, ed. Bob Perelman [Carbondale: Southern Illinois University Press, 1985], 230–45).

23. Robert Grenier, *What I Believe Transpiration* / Transpiring Minnesota (Berkeley: O Books, n.d.).

24. In fact, the first section is a reprint of a magazine-pamphlet publication, *Abacus*, and includes the magazine letterhead on its first page.

25. See the discussion of Allen Ginsberg's use of Pound's ideogram in Chapter Seven. See also Chapter Two of *The Trouble With Genius*.

26. I have reproduced pages 27 and 65. The page numbers are handwritten on the back of the paper, very faintly, in green pencil.

27. Barrett Watten, "Grenier's *Sentences*" in *L-A-N-G-U-A-G-E* 5 (New York: October, 1978), n.p.

28. William Wordsworth, "The Prelude," in *William Wordsworth (The Oxford Authors)*, ed. Stephen Gill (Oxford: Oxford University Press, 1984), 464.

Chapter Four

1. While I will use his analysis and writing in my initial discussion, I should point out that, in addition to group cohesiveness, there is also a parataxis of individuals within a group so that in some ways what Silliman writes is precisely what others do not. A debate between Silliman and Leslie Scalapino over narrative and gender was an overt sign of this: Silliman wrote that

> Progressive poets who identify as members of groups that have been the subject of history—many white male heterosexuals, for example—are apt to challenge all that is supposedly 'natural' about the formation of their own subjectivity. That their writing today is apt to call into question . . . such conventions as narrative, persona and even reference can hardly be surprising. At the other end of the spectrum are poets who . . . have been [history's] objects. . . . These writers and readers—women, people of color, sexual minorities, the entire spectrum of the 'marginal'—have a manifest political need to have their stories told. That their writing should often appear much more conventional, with the notable difference as to whom is the subject of these conventions, illuminates the relationship between form and audience.

Scalapino took issue, writing that Silliman's use of "conventional" implied "inferiority"; that his argument was "authoritarian." Rather than exploding persona,

Silliman's *"critique* of the unified subject, . . . the concept of 'objectivity' *consti-tutes* a unified subject." She went on, "You have a Marxist narration. . . . You are defining innovation as the repository of white men who are supposedly free of connection. Even if they could be free of connection, why should they be? E.g., why would that be viewed as innovative? I'm defining narrative as 'constructing.'"

The debate can be found in *Poetics Journal* 9 (June 1991):51–68. Scalapino uses some of the phrases of this debate in "Orion." See *The Return of Painting, The Pearl, and Orion: A Trilogy* (San Francisco: North Point Press, 1991), 151–54. Scalapino's approach to narrative is not paratactic—it owes more to the meditative style that Gertrude Stein developed in works such as *The Geographical History of America*; but a comparison of Scalapino's prose with new sentence writing would be very worthwhile.

2. Ron Silliman, "The New Sentence," in the book of the same name (New York: Roof Press, 1987), 63–93.

3. Ron Silliman, "Disappeance of the Word, Appearance of the World," *The New Sentence*, op. cit., 14.

4. "The Chinese Notebook," in *The Age of Huts* (New York: Roof, 1986), 50, 59, 62, 66.

5. Eliot Weinberger, "A Note on *Montemora*, America & the World," *Sulfur* 20 (Fall 1987):197. See also the discussion of Charles Altieri's comments in Chapter Two.

6. Fredric Jameson, *Postmodernism, or, the Cultural Logic of Late Capitalism* (Durham: Duke University Press, 1991), 26.

7. Bob Perelman, *The First World* (Berkeley: This, 1981), 60.

8. George Hartley discusses "China" in *Textual Politics and the Language Poets* (Bloomington: Indiana University Press, 1989), 42–52.

9. Michael Blumenthal, "Today I Am Envying the Glorious Mexicans," in *The Morrow Anthology of Younger American Poets*, ed. Dave Smith and David Bottoms (New York: Quill, 1985), 95.

10. Ron Silliman, *Ketjak* (San Francisco: This, 1978), 17.

11. Charles Olson, "Projective Verse," in *Selected Writings*, ed. Robert Creeley (New York: New Directions, 1966), 16.

Olson's Creeley is echoing not just Valery, but Hegel. "The aesthetics of idealism grasps the work of art as a form/content unity. 'True works of art are such, precisely by the fact that their content and their form prove to be completely identical,' says Hegel." Peter Burger, *The Decline of Modernism*, trans. Nicholas Walker (University Park, PA: Penn State University Press, 1992), 45.

12. Michel Foucault, "Preface to Transgression," in *Language, Counter-Memory, Practice: Selected Essays and Interviews*, ed. Donald F. Bouchard, trans. Bouchard and Sherry Simon (Ithaca: Cornell University Press, 1977), 41–42.

13. Ted Berrigan, *The Sonnets* (New York: Grove Press, 1964), 20.

14. Compare Robert Grenier's reeanctment of Williams's "castigation of the sonnet," discussed in the previous chapter.

15. The impulse to map the global condition can make the phrases of Jameson's own sentences somewhat analogous to Silliman's new sentences:

A roomful of people, indeed, solicit us in incompatible directions that we entertain all at once: one subject position assuring us of the remarkable new global elegance of its daily life and forms; another one marvelling at the spread of democracy, with all those new 'voices' sounding out of hitherto silents parts of the globe or inaudible class strata (just wait a while, they will be here, to join their voices to the rest); other more querulous and 'realistic' tongues reminding us of the incompetences of late capitalism, with its delirious paper-money constructions rising out of sight, its Debt, the rapidity of the flight of factories matched only by the opening of new junk-food chains, the sheer immiseration of structural homelessness, let alone unemployment, and that well-known thing called urban 'blight' or 'decay' which the media wraps brightly up in drug melodramas and violence porn when it judges the theme perilously close to being threadbare.) Jameson, *Postmodernism*, op. cit., 375–76.

This sentence was called to my attention by Jim English's review of *Postmodernism* in *Postmodern Culture*, 1, no. 3 (May 1991). Comparing them to new sentences, English describes Jameson's sentences as follows:

They are often . . . "impossible" in the sense that the two-hundred-word aphorism is impossible. A . . . refusal of any posture of poeticism or transcendence, coexists improbably with the bravura and self-involvement of Jameson's idiolect. Polemic is put into virtual abeyance by the tendency to stray across various and incompatible discursive fields, "picking up" bits of language here and there, celebrating the syntactic detour. And yet polemic . . . always reappears at the next rest stop, only to be lost again in the joyous (or is it tiresome?) intensity, the weirdly inappropriate euphoria, of another Jamesonian sentence.

16. Barrett Watten has compared the use of quotidian details in Williams and Silliman: for Williams "the inconsequential is dramatized as a single moment of truth that is also ironic," but Silliman's use is "a much more radical, ongoing process of evaluation." When Silliman describes a plastic fork from MacDonalds, Watten sees the sentence as commenting "on larger social forms. Monopoly capitalism will produce many such forks, but there can be only one in the poem. . . . The only solution is for the poem to keep going." *Total Syntax* (Carbondale: Southern Illinois University Press, 1985), 109.

    See also Jeffrey T. Nealon's discussion of Williams and Watten in *Double Reading: Postmodernism after Deconstruction* (Ithaca: Cornell University Press, 1993), 139.

17. Especially in subsequent expanded versions of the sentence: "She was a unit in a bum space, she was a damaged child, sitting in her rocker by the window" [6, 7, 11, 18, etc]. I discuss these repetitions in a moment.

18. T. S. Eliot, "The Waste Land," in *The Complete Poems and Plays* (San Diego: Harcourt Brace Jovanovich, 1971), 39.

19. "Preface to the Second Edition" of *Lyrical Ballads*, in *William Wordsworth Selected Poetry*, ed. Mark Van Doren (New York: Random House, 1950), 679.

    Also, the description of London in Book Seven of *The Prelude*, especially lines 656–92.

    —All moveables of wonder from all parts
    Are here, Albinos, painted Indians, Dwarfs,

The Horse of Knowledge, and the learned Pig,
The Stone-eater, the Man that swallows fire,
Giants, Ventriloquists, the Invisible Girl,
The Bust that speaks, and moves its goggling eyes,
The Wax-work, Clock-work, all the marvellous craft
Of Modern Merlins, wild Beasts, Puppet-shows,
All out-o'-th'-way, far-fetch'd, perverted things,
All freaks of Nature, all Promethean thoughts
Of man;

20. *Fables of Aggression: Wyndham, the Modernist as Fascist* (Berkeley: University of California Press, 1979), 3. The Jamesonian "we" is an odd construction; he is exempting himself from the "we."

21. Jameson concludes "The Cultural Logic of Late Capitalism" with a similar gesture: "the new political art . . . will have to hold to the truth of postmodernism . . . the world space of multinational capitalism—at the same time at which it achieves a breakthrough to some as yet unimaginable new mode of representing this last" (54).

22. *Fables*, 7.

23. *Demo to Ink* (Tucson, AZ: Chax Press, 1992), 131, 50, 107. (The title indicates a collection of six books from Silliman's ongoing series, *The Alphabet*; *Demo* is the first of the six.)

24. In "Disappearance of the Word, Appearance of the World," Silliman writes that commodified language becomes inseparable from entertainment spectacles: "the consumer of a mass market novel such as *Jaws* stares at a 'blank' page (the page also of the speed-reader) while a story appears to unfold miraculously of its own free will before his or her eyes." *The New Sentence*, 13.

25. Schematically, the pattern of *Ketjak* looks like this, with each letter representing a sentence, and the uppercase letters representing a repeated sentence:

    a.
    A. b.
    A. c. B. d.
    A. e. C. f. B. g. D. h.

The opening pages of *Ketjak* do not quite conform to this scheme, though the bulk of the book does. Silliman's next book, *Tjanting* (Great Barrington: The Figures, 1981), uses a much more complex system involving Fibonacci numbers. See the Silliman issue of *The Difficulties* for an interview, where Silliman compares this structure to class struggle. In the discussion in Barrett Watten's talk, "Russian Formalism and the Present," Watten and David Bromige speak of *Ketjak* as a novel. Watten says, "Each sentence is a device . . . this is close to Shklovsky's characterization of Sterne. *Ketjak* is a typical novel in the tradition of *Tristram Shandy*." Bromige: "You find out more about each sentence as you go along, in the way that you find out more about a character." See *Hills* 6/7 (1980): 66.

26. *What* (Great Barrington: The Figures, 1988), pages given in the text.

27. Lyn Hejinian, *My Life*, 2d edition (Los Angeles: Sun & Moon Press, 1987), 47–48.

28. Lyn Hejinian, *Oxota: A Short Russian Novel* (Great Barrington: The Figures, 1991). Page numbers given in the text.

29. Ron Silliman, *What*, 40.
30. For instance: "In the evenings particularly we made notes and took dictation in anticipation of writing a short Russian novel, something neither invented nor constructed but moving through that time as I experienced it unable to take part personally in the hunting" (12). *Oxota* is Russian for "hunt."
31. Michael Davidson, Lyn Hejinian, Ron Silliman, and Barrett Watten, *Leningrad* (San Francisco: Mercury House, 1991), 124.
32. For a very funny, and ultimately serious, acting out of the consequences of trying to live as an artist amid the West's sea of objects, see Steve Benson's performance-talk, "Views of Communist China," in *Hills* 6/7 (1980): 74–103.
33. See *The Way of the World: The* Bildungsroman *in European Culture* (London: Verso, 1987).
34. I owe this observation to Dana Phillips.
35. Quoted in Alice Kaplan, "The American Stranger," *The South Atlantic Quarterly* (Winter 1992): 91.
36. Gustave Flaubert, *Bouvard and Pecuchet*, trans. T. W. Earp and G. W. Stoner (Westport: Greenwood Press, 1954), 166–67.
37. I wrote the poem after looking, not at a book of photographs as Jameson writes, but at some sort of Chinese primer containing simple four-color pictures of 'the world': family, kitchen, school, rivers, airports, and village festivals.

Chapter Five

1. John Cage, *A Year From Monday* (Middletown: Wesleyan University Press, 1967), 149.
2. There is an interesting irony in the fact that Bernstein's critique of mainstream tokenism, which I will discuss later in the chapter, can now be turned on him: he is quite often the writer selected when an example of language writing is needed by critics.
3. See Bernstein's *Content's Dream* (Los Angeles: Sun & Moon Press, 1986), 244–51, for discussion of this.
4. The poem ends:

> What more is there to do, except stay? And that we cannot do.
> And as a last breeze freshens the top of the weathered old tower, I turn
> my gaze
> Back to the instruction manual which has made me dream of Guadalajara.

> (*Some Trees* [Ecco Press: New York, 1978], 18.)

5. Elizabeth Bishop, "Poem," in *The Complete Poems 1927–79* (New York: The Noonday Press, 1991), 176.
6. See *Spring and All*: "The sea that encloses her young body / ula lu la lu / is the sea of many arms"; or a stanza of self-critique from *The Descent of Winter*: "There are no perfect waves / Your writings are a sea / full of misspellings and / faulty sentences. Level. Troubled." William Carlos Williams, *Imaginations*, ed. Walter Schott (New York: New Directions, 1970), 136, 235.
7. See the introduction to *Bending the Bow* (London; Jonathan Cape, 1971), ii, where

Duncan compares antiwar demonstrators to an unorthodox text despised by soldier-readers.

8. "A Poem Beginning With a Line from Pindar," in *The Postmoderns*, ed. Donald Allen and George Butterick (New York: Grove, 1982), 56.

9. Percy Bysshe Shelley, "A Defence of Poetry," in *The Selected Poetry and Prose of Percy Bysshe Shelley*, ed. Carlos Baker (New York: Modern Library, 1951), 496–97. Subsequent page references in the text.

10. Bernstein's *Veils*, A chapbook whose pages are light gray with an overlay of letters, furnishes a textbook illustration of this tendency. (Madison: Xexorial Editions, 1987). Edward Kamau Brathwaite, *X/Self* (Oxford: Oxford University Press, 1987), 80. Subsequent page references are given in the text.

11. Samuel Taylor Coleridge, *Biographia Literaria*, ed. James Engell and W. Jackson Bate (Princeton: Princeton University Press, 1983), 304.

12. Charles Bernstein, *Dark City* (Los Angeles: Sun & Moon Press, 1994), 23–24.

Chapter Six

1. *The L=A=N=G=U=A=G=E Book*, ed. Bruce Andrews and Charles Bernstein (Carbondale, IL: Southern Illinois University Press, 1984).

2. "Constitution / Writing, Language, Politics, the Body," in *L=A=N=G=U=A=G=E*, Volume 4 (*Open Letter*, Fifth Series, No. 1 [1982]), ed. Bruce Andrews and Charles Bernstein. Page numbers will be given in the text.

3. "Confidence Trick," the last section of *Give Em Enough Rope* (Los Angeles: Sun & Moon, 1987), the book prior to *I Don't Have Any Paper*, anticipates the rhetoric of the subsequent book.

4. Bruce Andrews, *Give Em Enough Rope*, 28.

5. Bruce Andrews, *Tizzy Boost* (Great Barrington, MA: The Figures, 1993), n.p.

6. Bruce Andrews, *I Don't Have Any Paper So Shut Up (or, Social Romanticism)* (Los Angeles: Sun & Moon Press, 1992). Subsequent page numbers in text.

7. Clark Coolidge and Larry Fagin, *On the Pumice of Morons* (Great Barrington: The Figures, 1993), n.p.

8. Jean-François Lyotard, *The Postmodern Condition: A Report on Knowledge*, trans. Geoff Bennington and Brian Massumi (Minneapolis: University of Minnesota Press, 1984), 82.

9. Quoted in Julia Kristeva, *Powers of Horror* (New York: Columbia University Press, 1982), trans. Leon S. Roudiez, 176.

10. See Linda Orr, "Céline, Jean Zay, and the Mutations of Hate," in *Céline, USA* (*South Atlantic Quarterly*, Vol. 93, No. 2 [Spring 1994]), 333–44; and Alice Kaplan, *French Lessons* (Chicago: The University of Chicago Press, 1993), 189.

11. Louis-Ferdinend Céline, *Conversations with Professor Y*, tr. Starford Luce (Hanover: University Presses of New England), 95.

Chapter Seven

1. Barrett Watten, "Russian Formalism and the Present," in *Total Syntax* (Carbondale: Southern Illinois University Press, 1985), 29. At the beginning of the talk, he opposes the Russian Formalist sense of the constructed literary fact to a nonreflective sense of " 'bigness' or 'Frank' [O'Hara]" (2). For a very different imagination

of—construction of—"Frank," one that owes something to the instigation of Watten's remark two decades previously, see the final chapter.

2. Barrett Watten, "Mode Z," *1–10* (San Francisco: This Press, 1980), 9.
3. See John Guillory's *Cultural Capital: The Problem of Literary Canon Formation* (Chicago: The University of Chicago Press, 1993), 85–93, for discussion of the common factors in two "locodescriptive poems": Gray's "Elegy in a Country Churchyard" and Wordsworth's "Tintern Abbey."
4. Jean Baudrillard, *Simulations*, trans. Paul Foss, Paul Patton, and Philip Beitchman (New York: Semiotext[e], 1983), 2.
5. Charles Olson, "Projective Verse," in *Selected Writing*, ed. Robert Creeley (New York: New Directions, 1966), 15–26.
6. *American Literature: A Prentice Hall Anthology*, Volume Two, Emory Elliott, General Editor (Englewood Cliffs, NJ: Prentice Hall, 1991), 928.
7. Jerome McGann, "Dialogue on Dialogue," in *A Poetics of Criticism*, ed. Juliana Spahr, Mark Wallace, Kristin Prevallet, Pam Rehm (Buffalo: Leave Books, 1994), 77. McGann is punning on Laura Riding's "Poet: A Lying Word" (in *The Poems of Laura Riding* [New York: Persea Books, 1980], 216).
8. The anthology note I quoted claimed Frost's art had two basic sources, iambic lines and colloquial speech. A line like Stafford's here, and such lines from "The Gift Outright" as "We were withholding from our land of living," show that there is no necessary harmony between the two.
9. *Contemporary American Poetry*, ed. Donald Hall (Baltimore: Penquin Books, 1967), 27. I discuss (attack) this poem in "The First Person" (*Hills* 6/7, the *Talks* issue, 1980); an excerpt is reprinted in *William Stafford: The Worth of Local Things*, ed. Tom Andrews (Ann Arbor: University of Michigan Press, 1993). Rae Armantrout parodies the poem in "Travelling Through the Yard" (*Precedence* [Providence: Burning Deck Press, 1985], 180).
10. In other poems, Stafford occasionallly deals with the most basic of Frost's elisions: Native Americans.
11. The staying power of the adjective "card-carrying"—Bush successfully damaged Dukakis in the 1988 election by calling him a card-carrying member of the ACLU—is an index of the fearful fascination that groups continue to trigger in the American rhetorical arena. Critical discomfort with the group nature of language writing is a subset of this. The card the successful American is to carry is the credit card, where—instead of poetic voice—name, number, and sometimes a picture keep financial individuality inviolate.
12. *The Morrow Anthology of Younger American Poets*, ed. Dave Smith and David Bottoms (New York: Quill, 1985). Armantrout's review is in *Poetics Journal* 6 (1986):141–44.
13. See *The Opening of the Field* (New York: New Directions, 1960), especially poems such as "Often I am permitted to return to a meadow," 7.
14. A questionnaire from one of Duncan's early poetry workshops contained the following questions:

> 1. Think of a page on which you are writing a poem as being also a map. Do you write the poem with or against the sun?
> 2. What other geographical observations can you make about this imagined page of writing?

> 3. Name three great conquerors in the history of man and compare their movements with the movements of writing on this page.

A major point of the workshops, and of Duncan's and Spicer's work, was that the spaces and the maps were esoteric. Quoted in *The Collected Books of Jack Spicer*, ed. Robin Blaser (Los Angeles: Black Sparrow Press, 1975), 358.

15. For discussion of the Spicer-Duncan-Blaser circle, see Michael Davidson's *The San Francisco Renaissance: Poetics and Community at Mid-century* (Cambridge: Cambridge University Press, 1989), and Maria Damon's *Dark End of the Street: Margins in American Vanguard Poetry* (Minneapolis: University of Minnesota Press, 1993).

16. *The Collected Books of Jack Spicer*, ed. Robin Blaser (Los Angeles: Black Sparrow Press, 1975), 217, 265.

17. "Wichita Vortex Sutra," in *Planet News* (San Francisco: City Lights Books, 1968), 166–67. Subsequent page references will be given in the text.

18. See Allen Ginsberg, *Improvised Poetics*, ed. Mark Robison (San Francisco: Anonym, 1971).

19. In *The Collected Poems of William Carlos Williams*: Vol. 1 (New York: New Directions 1986), 406.

20. In fact, old-fashioned writers are consigned to the wrong side. A figure who echoes the hysterical call for mass bombing is criticized primarily for the benighted state of his ethics and information; but there is also, I think, a small dig at the backwardness of his writing technology:

> Bomb China's 200,000,000
> cried Stennis from Mississippi
> I guess it was 3 weeks ago
>
> Holmes Alexander in Albuquerque Journal
> Provincial newsman
> said I guess we better begin to do that Now,
> his typewriter clacking in his aged office
> on a side street. (116)

My student Matthew Hart pointed out how pervasive the opposition between oral truth and printed falsehood is throughout the poem.

21. In *Houseboat Days* (New York: Viking, 1977). Subsequent page references are given in the text.

22. Andrew Ross, *The Failure of Modernism* (New York: Columbia University Press, 1986), 178.

23. Barrett Watten, *Progress* (New York: Roof, 1985), 48. Subsequent page references given in the text.

24. Interview with Michael Amnasan, in *Ottotole* 2 (Winter 1986–87):36. Subsequent page references given in the text.

25. Elsewhere in the interview, Watten says, "I'm not taking a distance from them, but the poem is in a sense plumbing the depths of its own negativity" (43). Contrary to his assertions of distance, during the extended discussion of this passage Watten brings in many highly charged personal references. See 40–50. Michael Davidson discusses this passage in "'Skewed by Design': From Act to Speech Act in Language-Writing," *Aerial* 8 (1995):241–46.

26. "Men and girls" echoes the end of "Letter 3" of *The Maximus Poems*, among other places in the poem, and reads as a critique of Olson's patriarchal presumption:

> Isolated person in Gloucester, Massachusetts, I, Maximus, address you
> you islands
> of men and girls

Charles Olson, *The Maximus Poems* (Berkeley: The University of California Press, 1983), 16.

27. There are a number of curses in *Progress*: i.e., "Ineffective, the curse returns. / I write, as in a mirror, / This present" (4); "I break the course of thought. . . . // A curse to avoid interruption / Of prose" (82); "Anyone is liable to be cursed, / And that is a cure for you" (112).

28. Quoted in *A Suite of Poetic Voices: Interviews with Contemporary American Poets*, ed. Manuel Brito (Santa Brigida, Canary Islands: Kadle Books, 1992), 177.

29. In an interview, Adrienne Rich speaks of "the Feminist Language poets," referring to Susan Howe, Rachel DuPlessis, Kathleen Fraser, Frances Jaffer. Given her association with *HOW(ever)*, Dahlen would fit in Rich's critical construct. *Adrienne Rich's Poetry and Prose*, ed. Barbara Charlesworth Gelpi and Albert Gelpi (New York: Norton, 1994), 270.

30. In "Forbidden Knowledge," *Poetics Journal* 4 (1984): 3.

31. In *Ecrits* (New York: Norton, 1977), 41.

32. "*A Reading*: A Reading," in *Writing/Talks*, ed. Bob Perelman (Carbondale: Southern Illinois University Press, 1985), 113.

33. Beverly Dahlen, *A Reading* 1-7 (San Francisco: Momo's Press, 1985). Page references given in text.

34. "Analysis Terminable and Interminable," in *Therapy and Technique* (New York: Collier, 1963), 270.

35. Julia Kristeva, *Desire in Language: A Semiotic Approach to Literature and Art*, ed. Leon S. Roudiez, trans. Thomas Gora, Alice Jardine, and Leon S. Roudiez (New York: Columbia University Press, 1980), 289-91.

36. For Mary Rowlandson, see "The Captivity and Restoration of Mrs. Mary Rowlandson," in *The Birth-Mark: Unsettling the Wilderness in American Literary History* (Hanover, NH: Wesleyan University Press, 1993), 89-130; for Hope Atherton, see "The Articulation of Sound Forms in Time," in *Singularities* (Hanover, NH: Wesleyan University Press, 1990), 1-38.

37. Susan Howe, *Singularities* (Hanover, NH: Wesleyan University Press, 1990), 41. Subsequent page references in the text.

38. Peter Quartermain, *Disjunctive Poetics: From Gertrude Stein and Louis Zukofsky to Susan Howe* (Cambridge: Cambridge University Press, 1992), 192. For more discussion of Howe's work, see, among a rapidly increasing array, Marjorie Perloff, "'Collision or Collusion with History': Susan Howe's *Articulation of Sound Forms in Time*," in *Poetic License: Essays on Modernist and Postmodernist Lyric* (Evanston, IL: Northwestern University Press, 1990), 285-96; George F. Butterick, "The Mysterious Vision of Susan Howe," *North Dakota Quarterly* 55 (Fall 1987):312-21; and Rachel Blau DuPlessis, "Whowe: An Essay on Work by Susan Howe," in *Sulfur* 20 (Fall 1987): 157-65.

39. Susan Howe, *The Non-Comformist's Memorial* (New York: New Directions, 1993), 49.

40. Rae Armantrout, *Necromance* (Los Angeles: Sun & Moon Press, 1991), 11.

41. Ibid., 7.

42. Ibid., 10.

43. Carla Harryman, *In the Mode Of* (La Laguna, Canary Islands: Zasterle Press, 1991), 22. Subsequent page references given in the text. Parts of *In the Mode Of* have subsequently appeared—in a different order—in Harryman's *There Never Was a Rose Without a Thorn* (San Francisco: City Lights Books, 1995).

44. Adrienne Rich, "Diving Into the Wreck," in *The Fact of a Doorframe* (New York: Norton, 1984), 163–64.

INDEX